"In *Words for Readers and Writers*, Larry Woiwode—one of our most compelling and important contemporary voices—illuminates his life and his experience as a writer-of-faith, as a writer within whom and within whose works a profound Christian belief resides. In these essays and interviews, Woiwode takes us into his interior life, offering artful meditations on the holy acts of reading and writing. Woiwode explores what it means to be a writer-in-Christ, to celebrate the durability and holiness of language, to work at that place where the imagination and the soul intersect and flower. We should listen earnestly to what Woiwode has to say."

Gregory L. Morris, Professor of American Literature, Penn State Erie; author, *A World of Order and Light* and *Talking Up a Storm*

"I knew that I was in for a treat the moment I looked at the table of contents, which reads like a tempting menu of topics. When I started to read the essays I was captivated by the energy of Woiwode's mind and even more by how widely read and broadly informed he is. To read this book is to receive a liberal education. I believe that this is one of Woiwode's best books."

Leland Ryken, former professor of English, Wheaton College; author, Christian Guides to the Classics series

"A book on craft, yes, but more a book on living, Larry Woiwode's *Words for Readers and Writers* in my library sits between Flannery O'Connor's *Mystery and Manners* and John Gardner's *On Becoming a Novelist*. Not since O'Connor has a writer put the reader in such comfortable and uncomfortable places at the same time."

G. W. Hawkes, Professor of English, Co-Director Creative Writing, Lycoming College; author, *Surveyor* and *Gambler's Rose*

"Few writers can match Larry Woiwode for craft and care. Sentence by beautiful sentence he traces the lineaments of thought, feeling, and experience. He inhabits the roles that life has given him, as writer and critic, father and husband, and Christian, with a constant difficult grace. I admire his writing deeply; it is always gratifying to be in its presence."

Alan Jacobs, Clyde S. Kilby Chair, Professor of English, Wheaton College; author, *The Pleasures of Reading in an Age of Distraction*

"The word 'words' and the name 'Woiwode' are not only similar sounding but are practically synonymous. Who better to parse the subject of words than Larry Woiwode, one of our country's ultimate wordsmiths?"

John L. Moore, author, *The Breaking of Ezra Riley* and *Take the Reins*

"Why do you write? Where does it come from? What sort of life is it, anyway? We badger our writers with those questions certain that living that close to fire must surely have taught them something. Woiwode has been asked those questions many times, over the years, and this volume collects a vigorous, various set of answers. While settings and interlocutors shift, Woiwode's core insight, quietly returned to, remains always the same. What is writing but faith expressing itself through love?— giving yourself over to that first stab of insight, spending yourself prodigiously for others, certain that the one who calls you has already given you all things. One can learn much here about reading and writing, but one can learn even more what it means to believe."

Thomas Gardner, Alumni Distinguished Professor of English, Virginia Tech; author, *John in the Company of Poets: The Gospel in Literary Imagination*

"I loved it. I'd like to read it again this weekend. The way Woiwode phrased things humbled me completely . . . . Lots of food for thought . . . "

Victoria, college student

"'Metaphor is the meditative center of a writer's inner universe.' That's just too cool. This essay got me reading sections aloud to my parents because I needed to gush about it with somebody. Woiwode's essays have been a great encouragement— artistically and spiritually."

Phoebe, college student

WORDS FOR READERS AND WRITERS

Also by Larry Woiwode

Novels
Beyond the Bedroom Wall
Born Brothers
Indian Affairs
Poppa John
What I'm Going to Do, I Think

Short Stories
The Neumiller Stories
Silent Passengers

Poems
Even Tide
Poetry North: Five Poets of North Dakota

Memoirs
A Step from Death
What I Think I Did

Non-fiction and Essays
Acts: A Writer's Reflections on Writing, the Church, and His Own Life
Aristocrat of the West: The Story of Harold Schafer
*Words Made Fresh**

For Young Adults
*The Invention of Lefse**

*recent publications of Crossway

"

WORDS

for

READERS

and

WRITERS

"

SPIRIT-POOLED DIALOGUES

LARRY WOIWODE

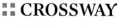
CROSSWAY

WHEATON, ILLINOIS

Crossway is a publishing ministry of Good News Publishers.

VP		23	22	21	20	19	18	17	16	15	14	13
15	14	13	12	11	10	9	8	7	6	5	4	3	2	1

For Laurel

Words, Words, Words,

that's life

The illusion of reality is a recurrent "idea" in Nabokov's fiction.
A lily, he once remarked, "is more real to a naturalist than it is
to an ordinary person. But it is still more real to a botanist.
And any further stage of reality is reached with that botanist
who is a specialist in lilies." In short, one gets closer to the
reality of an object the more intensely one studies it,
but no final or pure state of knowledge about lilies, or God,
or life, or the mysteries of nature can ever be attained.

PAGE STEGNER

Without minute neatness of execution
the sublime cannot exist.

WILLIAM BLAKE

CONTENTS

INTRODUCTION

The following essays formed an eerie architecture of meaning as I selected them from two drawers of a four-drawer file. The dialogues they record are both inner and outer, between me and memory and interviewers and editors. They deal with the act of writing, with a reader's response to writing, and the ways we all use words, including Facebook entries, to fashion meaning for our lives—even identities.

Words about writing, once on a page, form pooling metaphors that a reader can enter into in a dialogue. Recurring motifs reflect across the pools and a variety of meanings form a growing unity. This is abetted by a spirited gravity that sets them in pooling emphases.

If that's what writers feel when they say they're inspired, I feel and have felt inspired. The Spirit has pressed out a variety of views that counterbalance one another in the spirit-pooled dialogues of my title.

PART ONE

USES OF WORDS

1

ABCS THAT TEND TO FAMILY UNITY

a.

Settled families tend toward melodic unity. Unsettled families create alternating disharmony. A settled family atmosphere can arrive by finding a place to live, one agreeable to both parents, if both are present to weave their baritone-bass and contralto among the melodies of piping offspring. The voices of children affect a family's composition and establish the countermelodies the children's lives will assume as they mature and move on. All family members carry secrets in an unvoiced region at the center of their selves—a symphonic and hidden second home to each.

The pressures of the unvoiced region can cause family members to broaden their understanding, first for one another and then for an interrelated community, forming works from words that include others—*the* other. Healthy members situate even the unappealing in their interiors, from the Grimm or Disney characters of childhood to the Ophelias and Othellos of an adult. Members release ghosts and welcome guests who gather in the sunny or leaf-speckled spheres of their hidden interiors.

These are the characters of bedtime stories or tales of Grandpa growing up. Collections of stories gather inside family boundaries in a compression of artistic collaboration that encourages expression.

Stories form a family's outlook, whatever its origin or ethnicity or age or character, and this outlook is apparent in a family's ability to use language and in the gestures and the poses their bodies take on.

That is why children—and those who grow into parents—page through albums of family photographs. The fixed and still gestures suggest further routes into the inner self of the family, over paths leading to the past from the present. The ground note underneath, informing integration, is *place*. When a family needs to define a gap or find what's lost, they return to the *place* where their thought began—from the basement of forgetfulness to the kitchen or computer desk.

Place is the home base for both hide-and-seek and philosophical speculation. Both need a binding origin to begin. Both use words in their countdown. A common bond is that all houses and apartments, invested with the artwork of family stories, resound with a variety of routes for each member. The source of resonance is the historical base of the stories families tell. They construct personages and place them in phenomenal existence. That's the primary use of words.

b.

My wife and I introduced to existence, in this order: daughter, son, daughter, daughter. I hoped to be a father to all, not a patriarch or rival, and before any were able to speak I began to carve a separate space to meet with each. Photos exist of the four, from their early months, sitting in my lap beside an open book I'm reading from. I didn't use reading as a means of setting my seal on their consciousness—the stories weren't mine—but as a way of assembling for them, through the metaphor of words, a pleasant and reassuring space where the two of us—or more if I was reading to more than one—might meet.

The meeting place was specific and objective or, if not quite objective—my wife and I chose the books—benign to their forming personalities and not crowded with parental rule. As an adult I could contain the content of a children's book and in that way establish a realm where each child could rest. One would cling to my shirt, another grab at my lips or hair or the skin of my cheek, imprinting my person on them, I presume, as provider of an external habitation that held a story containing us in its weave.

Each one could enter and strobe the substance of that story in his or her way, while as reader I was merely a medium providing a slip-step to a safe state. The jaded or squeamish or overly worried parent might wonder whether reading-in-the-lap is too intimate. Don't worry; be happy! Its benefits outweigh outmoded fears.

I write stories and novels, where all is metaphor, aware that the cultivation of metaphor can be a trying occupation. When our children were growing up, I was often so immersed in my work I had to rise from it like a deep-sea diver from ocean depths to keep from inflicting the bends of my mind—overly mature or unfamiliar emotion—on my children or, worse, drawing them into the undefined underworld I was exploring, word by word, as an adult. These are stories that our children, as children, never heard.

Gerald Locklin, a poet who enjoys a day out with his daughter, says,

> When we get home I am smart enough
> To downplay to my wife what a good day
> We have had on our own. Later, saying
> Goodnight to my little girl,
>
> Already much taller than her mother,
> I say, "days like today are the favorite
> Days of my life," and she knows
> It is true.[1]

Parents can speak of love for a child that wholeheartedly, as long as it's not habitual, because children are guiltless of a past history of disagreement or agenda, hidden or otherwise. Children are guiltless even of their birth.

C.

Young adults who find fault with their parents or harbor negative views about a parent have difficulty keeping out of trouble. A primary reason is lack of intimacy with a parent. A young adult's criterion of judgment is often cultural, most of which originates outside the family, at school or on a playing field or in a mall or on Facebook, and has less to do with the character of a parent than with the values of friends. And when values overtake morals, chaos has come again.

A father who does not communicate with his family, however, no matter the views he holds or, worse, who inflicts the silent treatment on a daughter or a son, is on the road to enrolling himself as a target of disdain. A mother may ameliorate that, but eventually the father has to engage in a juggling act to keep his relationship to his children from loosening into the disruptive clatter of free fall.

The way to keep those routes or, better, *highways* of communication open is by reading to a child from the beginning of his or her perceptions. A developing child experiences your voice forming the shape of a story, the story unites you as one, and in that unity a child learns to listen and respond to your voice. Finally, a father must listen to the newest story from a variety of sources that rise in the voices of his children.

The experience of listening to a child's story is a parent's aid to newfound perception. My wife and I encouraged communication in our children, and I'm surprised at how they keep in touch. One or another phones or texts or sends e-mails daily, asking our opinion or advice or merely wondering about their stand in the present. We speak to them from the realm first formed by the stories they heard us read over the years when they, and we, too, were growing up.

2

READERS' LITERARY
GUIDE TO LITIGATION

It may seem odd, or perhaps revelatory, that Henry James and Robert Louis Stevenson developed a close relationship, largely by correspondence. James was acknowledged as the superior artist, although Stevenson was no slouch, and their bond seems the sort that occurs in opposites. The lesson of their relationship, with its several different angles, is a lesson practicing lawyers might attend to, and I don't mean in choosing clients.

A distillation of that relationship can be found in Graham Greene's essay, "Two Friends." Greene is reviewing a biography of Stevenson by Janet Adam Smith and in its midst shifts to an examination of the friendship that developed between the two writers.[1] The biography of Stevenson, "sees in the friendship the aesthetic appeal to James of Stevenson's situation":

> The man living under the daily threat of a fatal hemorrhage, yet with such an appetite for the active life; the novelist who could only gain the health and energy for writing at the risk of dissipating them on other ends; the writer who had to spur his talent to earn more and more money to pay for the life of action that kept him alive; the continual tug between the claims of life and literature—here was a situation not unlike those which had provided James with the germ of a novel or story.

This glimpse of Stevenson could as well be a thumbnail sketch of a high-powered, occasionally reckless litigator.

James, on the other hand, once he moved from the security of the family brownstone on Washington Square, off Fifth Avenue, to England, maintained the reserved and distant (some thought cold) composure that perhaps only an expatriate writer with no financial worries in the world can adopt. He seemed comfortable only at his writing desk, and is the exact person one would want to work on contracts and briefs. His weighty seriousness, as Greene points out, was no match for Stevenson's agile metaphors, as in a moment in their correspondence when Stevenson confronted James on the inability of fiction to compete with life:

> These phantom reproductions of experience, even at their most acute, convey decided pleasure, while experience itself, in the cockpit of life, can torture and slay.

One can imagine the effect of this poised and colorful statement in a courtroom, where "phantom reproductions of experience" are recounted, some of which may include a torture or a slaying. In a mode more instructive, perhaps, Stevenson writes to James that "catching the very note and trick, the strange irregular rhythm of life, *that* is the attempt whose strenuous force keeps Fiction upon her feet."[2] It is the tricky capture of the note of "the strange irregular rhythm of life" that will enable the lawyer as communicator to keep listeners, especially a jury, alert.

But it was James who proved more relevant to courtroom procedure, and not for his rolling, periodic sentences or fine-tuned sensibility. James nailed down for all artful communication that would follow the concept of *point of view*. Before his strictures, narrators of fiction were often omniscient or the point of view shifted from epistle to epistle in the earliest novels or from character to character or scene to scene, as with Fyodor Dostoyevsky and Leo Tolstoy and later their American counterparts. James said in more than one preface (and in his practice) that a novel or story that begins in third person point of view must adhere to that point of view in every movement to its end, for aesthetic and conceptual veracity to adhere.[3]

His view arrived with such intellectual weight that by the 1940s and 1950s into the 1960s, American writers and instructors of creative writing were talking noisily as telegraphers about *violation* of point of view, as if it were an imbedded law about the human body.

The points of view can be summarized in simple fashion: *first person*, meaning "I did this, I did that," the *I—I—I* of too many modern novels; *second person*, meaning "You were the one, you did that," seldom used for a novel although long stories have been composed using it; *third person*, meaning "She did that, he did this," the mode commonly used in distanced writing of a Jamesian mode; *limited third*, meaning "She or he is I"—that is, limited within the skull of the same, singular person—an effect similar to first person, when handled judiciously; and *omniscient*, meaning "I am like God" in that I maintain an all-seeing overview of every mortal within my weather below, as epitomized in Thomas Hardy. The shifting Tolstoyan view, however, often accommodates all of the above, excluding the first person "I" that entered with Ivan Turgenev and Anton Chekov.

These compartmentalized limits, as they may be seen, must be adhered to in a courtroom. The defendant is always "he" or "she," unless he takes the stand, and in that movement takes on the first person "I," as in "I did not do that"—although she may include references, within limits that don't extend to hearsay or impugning others, in the third person: "*He* did it."

The litigator, in referring to this witness, must be solicitous to use the second person, as in, "Is it true that you . . ." Occasionally this litigator may step back inside his or her first person to say, "I think that you . . ." but this step is best taken with prudence or is likely to summon the first person response, "I object, Your Honor!" The only situation in which a litigator may safely use the first person singular ("we" is the province of judge and jury) is when he is called to the bench to explain himself, as in the instance of using first person too freely in interrogations.

Your Honor, the judge and court, must be addressed in third person, to signify his or her objective distance, excluding an advocate for the lowly who spurns unseemly excuses, such as Judge Judy, and is often referred to in an elevated third that suggests an omniscient entity, as in "If it please the Court . . . " The court, the judge, is permitted to use any person she pleases: "You, sir, are out of order," or "I rule that . . ." or "She may retake the stand," or "This Court, having reviewed the arguments for introducing evidence . . ."

If the lawyer-litigator does not mind his manners to remain inside the circumscribed points of view set solidly in place in American fiction by Henry James, then that lawyer, though he might ascend to the colorful language and stories of Robert Louis Stevenson, had best exempt himself from another day in court.

3

THE WORDED FLOOD,
RURAL TO ACADEMY

Poetry was my pursuit in high school, and in 1960 I enrolled at the University of Illinois, Urbana, with 35,000 students in residence, plus a meager number who met on a pier in Lake Michigan—the Navy Pier Chicago branch. The Urbana population formed a community, mostly cohesive, and it was there that my faith faded and went underground for a decade.

Agnosticism and atheism and a welter of other *isms*—more than words to those who encounter them in their youth—including some I'd never heard of, were in the air along with whiffs of smoke with the scent of burning leaves. Professors and graduate assistants held forth at the front of classrooms from oak lecterns that had the appearance of sawed-off upper halves of pulpits. They set these on their desks at the front of the room, chopping the church in two and taking over, puffing on pipes or cigarettes as they spoke.

It was a new religion they preached.

A Big Man on Campus ("B-Moc," in that era's lingo), the sort who wore a suit and tie and topcoat and was campaigning for the office of president of the student senate, stopped me one day in the corridor of Lincoln Hall, used by many as a passageway between the journalism and English buildings, and said, "You must be Woiwode, right?"

"Yes."

"It looks like you're a real existentialist," he said, naming one of the *isms* I hadn't heard of.

"Oh?" I said, wary, and felt the red flag of an entity I couldn't define start fluttering. *Existentialism?*

"You know, Camus and Sartre and those guys. I mean, those poems of yours!" They had appeared in a campus publication. "They're existential, man, if anything is! Keep it up!" I was flattered, of course, even if I didn't know what the word meant, and nobody I asked could give a satisfactory definition. But I wonder now, with sobering shots of cynicism added to my outlook, if he wasn't fishing for a vote.

A professor of mine, an impeccable and widely published scholar with a sweet sense of humor, a true gentleman, referred to people of faith as "Christers," as in "That Christer!"—dissing them, as we say now. It hurt at first to hear that word from a dear person otherwise so tolerant and kind, and then I fell into his fashion—or anyway imagined the label amused rather than included me.

Nobody told me you need faith to write poetry—some larger view to draw the arrangement of words free from mere verbal construction, no matter how technically sound or pyrotechnic, into the realm where they sail off in song. I enrolled in an advanced course in the metaphysical poets—John Donne, George Herbert, and Andrew Marvell—because one of the draws was the instructor. He glowed with intelligence and was lively and witty, able to cause students hardened by groveling study to laugh. I preferred the precise and subtly dodging movements of his mind revealed in his lectures to my generally flat-footed method of getting at matters, but I grew disenchanted with the class. I couldn't imagine why I was troubled about it. For a while I found it difficult to attend, and sometimes didn't.

Was it because he never mentioned that the poets he assigned to study were applying their faith or singing in ecstasy out of its holy strictures? I was drawn to the poets, pulled into their worlds on my own, but I don't recall any explanations about what it was that captivated their intellects or generated the force behind their poetry—other than, as the professor said, they followed the form of metaphysical conceit or extended metaphor to the breaking point, and so forth.

Let me confess that I did well in science but wasn't the sophisticate fit for literary study. What I probably needed to hear was "They wail in faith, baby!" One of the lows in my academic life came when I submitted a paper to this instructor on Marvell. I worked it over in my dogged way and received a grade of C, with this explanation: "Good as far as it goes but needs detail." I asked the professor what details he meant, since my paper was mostly details, and the fellow I found so witty frowned at me in a frosty way, and said, "You can't possibly know. You didn't attend all my lectures."

I hope this doesn't seem a disaffected student taking a poke at a professor who gave him a C. I've been a professor and know the theme. I admired him as much as the Christer professor but he helped define an angle of the atmosphere of the sixties—the "Me Generation" about to implode over the United States and then the globe, as if "I" and "me" were the only entities able to provide proper answers. That was the animating religion behind most of the poetry I read a decade later.

What I needed was a collection like *A Sacrifice of Praise* with a discerning and gentle guide like James Trott.[1] In his anthology readers will find what I was able to only suspect in some small area sovereignly preserved in me: that the tradition in Western literature is Christian.

Arbiters of consensus and taste, let's call them, who are drawn from the academic community, tend to overlook this historical statistic. They would like to expunge any suggestion that God appeared incarnate on the earth, in the person and realm that the poets in Trott's collection celebrate. Academics have been scrupulous to alter even AD (the Latin *anno Domini*, meaning "in the year of our Lord") to CE, Common Era.

No matter how you change the name of centuries of artistry, however, or sift the entries in the pantheon of poets of the past, you always arrive at an unassailable truth: the tradition in Western literature is Christian.

You see glimmers of it in *Beowulf* (Verses added by a monk? Who can say a monk didn't write *Beowulf?*) and then the métier arrives full-blown in Chaucer, with subject matter unclouded by Victorianism—which has no part in Christianity and dampens the appreciation of poetry for present-day Christians. The subject and object of the body is holy to God, the sacrifice of praise Christians are expected to offer, as Christian painters down the centuries have done. I know of Christian writers criticized in their community for using words like "naked"—a word the Bible leans on. If that's your view, watch out for Chaucer, lock up Donne, banish husband-clinging Anne Bradstreet, expunge portions of T. S. Eliot, and keep an eye out for those doubled metaphors in Emily Dickinson, and please, please, please, steer clear of that master of double entendre, William-the-bard-from-Avon Shakespeare.

But, dear reader, I expect better of you, and propose you take Trott as your guide and with him meet the magnificent residents of *A Sacrifice of Praise*—centuries of poets with Christ at their center. It's a commendable work Trott has arranged, and you'll find Sauls and Jepthahs present, engaged in a hope that the highest reach of their words will touch the hem of the Word.

Two decades ago I was working on a novel and hit a stretch when the words ran like cream—a dozen pages or so. I usually write in pencil, anyway for my first draft, but that afternoon I was at a computer, because of time constraints and who knows what, diving through a section of action that had me so engaged I couldn't pause to hit the "save" button, a necessary adjunct to word processing then, when a lightning bolt hit.

Out went the computer and the twelve pages dissolved in a sinking dot on the screen. This had happened before and I knew that with all the well-intentioned effort I might summon, I could never recapture the onrush of words as they had arrived. It wouldn't do any good to turn on God or shake my fist at the electric company. By a *force majeure* the pages were gone, and perhaps a swift distillation would be better—or so I was trying to persuade myself to think. No hope of the electricity appearing seemed in the offing, in the midst of the thunderous downpour the arid high plains often receive on a sweltering summer day. We lived twelve miles from the nearest town, dependent on the fallible intricacies of rural electricity. So I followed the impulse of my children, donned rubber boots and a slicker, and went out to enjoy this visitation on our parched land. I'm not sure I've been in a rain that heavy. I felt I was under a cataract, the weight of the water over my rain gear adding greater gravity to any movement I made. Runnels and rivulets were appearing where I'd never seen water, forcing grass flat, sliding down our lane, turning it slick, while ditches everywhere I looked were running clay-yellow and red-brown. The pour of rain increased, and a narrow creek at the bottom of our pasture, usually dry at that time of year, was spreading so wide it started to climb the incline of the pasture that bordered it.

According to a later news report we had six inches of rain in an hour. A gravel road runs between our pasture and the pasture of a neighbor, down an incline from our lane, and a mile and a half into his fields a hogback butte rears up two hundred feet high for a good mile. I heard runoff from the butte hit the already pouring water in the pasture across the road and told our children to move to higher ground, and then it came, a rumbling sea wave that hit the road with a tsunami crash and started boiling in a rise to gain its top, the road banked high here for a bridge that spans our usually dry creek.

The pressure of the water sent a fifty-foot column shooting through the arch of the bridge, raising the water level in our pasture as fast as we could watch. It didn't seem the bridge could handle the onslaught and, sure enough, the water surged to the level of the road and started slithering over its top, then came pouring over the raised length of it in a thundering waterfall. Our children were young enough to cheer and their voices helped me weigh my lost pages against this force of nature.

All the interconnected technology that I and others depended on every day was insignificant compared to this—a ripple across the thousand inventions over the centuries. No matter how much I might prepare to preserve what we had, and no matter the effort engineers and road builders installed in the local landscape to direct the aftermath of rains and melts and floods, nothing could contain a force of this magnitude that was up to do what it would do.

And nothing can contain the outpour of poetry that carries us on a current to the source of the power of words, as the uncontained cataract seemed the worded flood of tradition pouring down to us out of centuries past, and no degree of denial or patronizing or belittling or exclusion could keep it from pouring in thunderous collusion to the glory of its origins into centuries to come.

4

AUTOBIOGRAPHY, BIOGRAPHY, FICTION, AND FACT

At the beginning of 1999 I sent off, for the last time, a biography that took four years to finish. I had estimated it would take two. During the third year, the manuscript rose to a thousand pages and finally ended at five hundred. My experience should be a warning to anybody who has worked in nearly every form of writing, as I had, except biography, and is tempted to try.

I was tempted because of a commission, and my interest in the subject of the biography. He was the founder of Gold Seal, the distributor of Snowy Bleach and Mr. Bubble for starters—able to boast that every American household at one time held two of his products, based on number of sales. He shook hands with or befriended every American president from Herbert Hoover to George H. W. Bush. His son Ed served two terms as governor of North Dakota. Above all, he was a Christian gentleman who gave away millions to anybody who asked: Harold Schafer.

Before I get into the genres of writing in my title, all of which touch on the actuality of life, I want to glance at a topic that has most Americans in its grip: money. I've had well-intentioned, intelligent people say to me, "You mean you write for money?" They might as well ask a teacher if she teaches for a paycheck—or ask that of most. Teachers teach because they love to, I assume, as my father did, and receive pay as workers worthy of their hire.

"But how can you accept a huge amount as an advance on a book you haven't even started yet?" Or "How can you agree to do a piece of so many words for x amount of dollars in x amount of time?"

These are questions I'm asked and I need to say, first, I don't remember the advance as so huge. The questions come from a perspective that assumes the marketplace sullies creative pursuits. Another side to this can get tortuous. I was attending a conference in Chicago and met a pastor who asked, "What do you do?"

I was beginning to develop a resistance to admit what I did, because of the responses I tended to get, especially in the churchgoing world I had recently merged with. But I was also aware, as a writer, that lying is not a salubrious trait.

"I write," I said.

"Write?"

"Books."

"What does your wife do?"

"She proofreads and offers suggestions." I nodded at my wife, who was holding our infant son in her arms. "She's my best critic and a wonderful intellect and mother."

"Is she independently wealthy?" he asked.

"No."

"Are you?"

"No."

"Then how can you write?"

I feel no shame at being paid for my work and, like any professional, I bank on that. Besides, every writer is working against a deadline, whether imposed by an editor or grocer or landlord or the IRS or the ultimate deadline, death.

When I was introduced to the material gathered on the subject of the biography I was asked to write, stacked in overflowing boxes in a forty-by-twenty storage room, I said, "Goodness, this is going to take at least two years."

"Well," the president of the foundation who hired me said, "you have one."

That it took four years is proof that all deadlines aren't met. The foundation decided to fund one year of the work with no archivists, no librarians, no research assistants, no assistance. A fortuitous gift to my wife helped us through another year, and an annuity of mine two more—to return to the pastor's question of how writing is funded, and to my early topic, money.

A major difficulty with the biography, as I look back with a sigh of freedom, wasn't just the mass of materials—thousands of pages, for instance, merely of transcribed interviews—but a sensation I had never experienced that seemed to creep from my feet to my fingers in an enveloping grip: I had to secure every sentence with a counterweight of appropriate facts. Sometimes I checked half a dozen sources or variants on a story in order to draft a single page.

My experiential sense of this was the need to keep my sentences from rolling away on their own, so the feelers of their words would grip, as it were, the shape of the facts, and the sentences grip the page. I realized, too, that in a certain sense these weren't facts—the moments the person of the biography experienced were indisputable for him (and me)—and any reconstruction of those, using any of the genres of my title, was a metaphor, a recapturing of a state *in words*.

As you see, I've been indulging in autobiography. If anybody decides to write about my mention of this project, that could be biography, or if you wanted to include the matrix of the year this moment is rising from, it might better be fiction. Each of the genres uses the form of metaphor to deliver its "facts."

No fact exists without an interpretation of it, as a philosopher by the name of Cornelius Van Til once said. What he meant is if I say, "The Civil War," anybody who hears those words is stormed by separate sets of facts, some merely by my naming it as I have. If you view it as a war of northern aggression, you have facts to support that. If another sees it as a conflict that installed commercial manufacture over agrarian interests, facts might well support that view. If I say its genesis was slavery, I might be closer to the truth, but I would have to summon my series of facts to support that.

Look at a less controversial fact: *tree.* A different tree may come to mind for each, but if we can agree on one tree, a birch, say, standing separate against a green landscape, what we know or are able to observe will govern our description of the facts about the birch that each of us sees.

Take a step farther back. If you believe trees are the result of random happenstance or believe they were ordained to look as they do, part of a design fulfilled, then your view of the tree and facts about it will differ, according to your ideology. One may end up a tree hugger, as it's put, gripping the birch as if it's a god, another an ecologist studying the relationship of this birch to an indigenous ecological system—a "tree" among the interrelationships at the heart of the reason the universe continues to cohere.

A further complication of the biography I was working on was that the subject was in full health, in Technicolor, in his eighties. His personality kept shifting into further potentials that seemed fitting paths to follow to describe him. What he was in the world had not been sealed off as it usually is at death. So my idea of exactly who the essential persona of this person was—even that idea altered.

When I say "Civil War" or "tree," if the words have no more meaning to you than a post, or none at all, then my arrangement of the "facts" will define the phenomenon for you and, in a sense, you're at my mercy. This happens with the words of self-promotion that politicians employ until life-practices intervene.

Finding the right words to describe a person is *true to a far greater degree*, since each person is endowed with many dimensions, some hidden. When writers arrive at a definition, it's because their thoughts form or slip into a metaphor that feels suitable. The thoughts may not be entirely clear at first or, if they are, the writer may not know in which genre to cast the accumulating words.

Factual work can be inaccurate or assembled to deceive. Fiction can be more factual than nonfiction. These are the facts.

I learned that the checking department at the *New Yorker* is or was as scrupulous about fiction or a "casual," as fiction was called, as a "fact piece." A phrase "the Willet subdivision in San Jose" appeared in a story of mine, and a checker wrote in a margin, "There is a San Jose in the area of Illinois where the story is set, with an x-and-x subdivision, and there is an x-and-x Willet in a nearby town of Manito, but there is no Willet subdivision in San Jose. Does author know this?"

Yes, I did, and I switched names and details to keep from implicating any person or town while retaining the local color—words indigenous to the area with local resonance—San Jose, for instance, in its central Illinois form, pronounced San *Joze.*

An awful urge for accuracy animates authors of fiction. You see it across the spectrum, from Eudora Welty to Vladimir Nabokov to John Updike to Annie Dillard to David Foster Wallace. It's a trait that can send a writer into a tailspin of hours or days to confirm a fact before moving to the next paragraph, rather than plowing ahead and straightening out the details later, as a biographer—a writer of facts, one assumes—assured me was the way he worked. He wrote the story first, he said, and fitted in the facts later.

The urge for the absolute animates writers of fiction because it's *their* truth that's on the line, not a "fact" from *Britannica* or a reference from yet another biography that to an auditor other than the author might seem to have a slant so steep it could be called "spin." So any serious writer of fiction feels from head to toe a tremor similar to an earthquake when somebody who isn't familiar with the process says they don't have time for fiction because they prefer only real facts.

On the E-Channel website, Charles Johnson answered a question from an inquisitor nearly every day of the year over 2011, and in a post for June 1 (only partially reproduced here), he tallies some of the potentialities of fiction:

> In an article published thirty-one years ago in *Obsidian*, "Philosophy and Black Fiction" (1980), I argued that "the final concern of serious fiction is the liberation of perception." I also stated in that article that, "our experience as black men and women completely outstrips our perception—black life is ambiguous and a kaleidoscope of meanings, rich, multi-sided, and what the authentic black writer does is despoil meaning to pin down the freshest interpretation given to him. This is genuine fiction. It is also hermeneutic philosophy, in the sense that the writer is an archaeologist probing the Real for veiled sense."
>
> In her often-cited work *Love's Knowledge* (1990), philosopher Martha Nussbaum says, "In a sense Proust is right to see the literary text as an 'optical instrument' through which the reader becomes a reader of his or her own heart." . . . Nussbaum continues, saying, "One obvious answer was suggested by Aristotle: we have never lived enough. Our experience is, without fiction, too confined and too parochial . . ."
>
> "The point," says Nussbaum, "is that in the activity of literary imagining we are led to imagine and describe with greater precision, focusing our attention on each word, feeling each event more keenly—whereas much of actual life goes by without that heightened awareness, and is thus, in a sense, not fully or thoroughly lived."
>
> The late John Gardner offered a similar vision of fiction in *On Moral Fiction*. There, he states, "In fiction we stand back, weigh things as we do not have time to do in life; and the effect of great fiction is to temper real experience, modify prejudice, humanize . . ."[1]

Gardner further enumerates the artistic and cultural roadblocks a writer of fiction faces in *On Moral Fiction*:

> We need to stop excusing mediocre and downright pernicious art, stop "taking it for what it's worth" as we take our fast foods, our overpriced cars that are no good, the overpriced houses we take all our lives fixing, our television programs, our schools thrown up like barricades in the way of young minds, our brainless fat religions, our poisonous air, our incredible cult of sports, and our ritual of fornicating with all pretty or even horse-faced strangers. We would not put

up with a debauched king, but in a democracy all of us are kings, and we praise debauchery as pluralism.[2]

Let me return to the monetary compensation for writing. It adds to the sense of accomplishment when the work is done and on its way into the world. But no joy surpasses the joy a writer feels as the work moves ahead and strives for the form that was present in a writer's mind before even beginning to set down words to encapsulate that form. And there's no accomplishment comparable to giving oneself over to a book entirely, as its servant. A glorious dimension—and I mean this in a literal sense—is when the work serves the one who put the love for form in one's mind and coaxes out passages that are so irrefutable, later, that they appear to shine in italics, once spirited gravity presses the accumulating words into pooling emphases.

I've indulged in autobiography and given inside information on a biography, and now I want to draw the threads of these genres together as a novelist would—not through the braided rope of narrative but a wiggly line of present thought: I said if you wrote about this moment later, that would be biography; if you wanted to deliver the whole of the moment within a dramatic context, that would be fiction. And if I decided to make a story of it or add it as a scene to a novel, that would be autobiographical fiction—a form that employs actual elements from a particular person's life at a literal time and becomes "auto" by the ultra-personal focused "I" of its metaphor. A novel along these lines is traditionally called a *roman à clef*.

I first heard the term "autobiographical fiction" from William Maxwell. He was an alumnus of the University of Illinois, and in the year I heard him, 1963, he was asked to speak at a yearly "Arts Festival"—ahead of rock festivals, but the same idea, and with as many in attendance in the sixties as at early rock festivals. He titled his talk "The Autobiographical Novelist," and spoke from personal experience, I presumed, because he had by then published five novels, most with a tang of "from his life."

He was known as an editor of, well, autobiographical fiction, and

37

had worked with J. D. Salinger, Eudora Welty, John Cheever, John Updike, and a dozen other semi-autobiographical writers. He spoke in a
diffident, whispery voice, difficult to hear in an auditorium, and all at
once said, "The autobiographical novelist is the sort of person who
can stand at his mother's coffin and notice the shape his shoes are in."[3]

I don't remember a word he said after. In that sentence I was defined. I had done that.

Who I would be was named, although it took years of experimenta-
tion with different forms and genres to understand his definition, and
it's a discovery I find difficult to admit, even now. Readers (and critics)
tend to dismiss the artistry of this kind of fiction, an aspect Maxwell
didn't mention in his talk. Readers suspect and even say, "This guy
hasn't got enough imagination to invent or make up stories so he robs
his own life."

Novelists are supposed to be creative and *inventive*, certain readers
seem to assume, although invention is the most rudimentary tool of
the rankest amateur, and the more fantastical the invention the more
"creative," even *valid*, a writer is. That trend, however, has recently
been driven aside by the outpour of memoirs.

Those words of Maxwell rest in balance with another attitude I've
mentioned, which I'll put in an imaginary mouth: "I don't have time to
read novels. I only read facts. I like to read what's real, not what guys
like you make up." So writers can catch it from both sides, and both
sides illustrate how seldom readers grant factual gravity to the artfully
assembled words tradition has come to call fiction.

No genre or form has the power to present a dimensional sense of
the world as a novel does, as Charles Johnson has said, because

> perception-liberating art is the antithesis of ideology, clichéd think-
> ing, the unimaginative, and works that do no more than recycle pre-
> established or second-hand meanings and interpretations of our
> experience. Real fiction makes the familiar *un*familiar. It shakes up
> calcified ways of seeing. It activates in us a Beginner's Mind, as Bud-
> dhists would say. And we can never again think of a subject, event or

experience without recalling the work of art—the gift—that caused scales to fall away from our eyes.[4]

This definition doesn't even enter the dimensions included in character. These range far deeper and far above the imagistic jittering of film and TV. The cultural and philosophical and historical implications of a novel from a past century (to step aside from the present) and its multiple layering of realities, as in Dostoyevsky's *The Brothers Karamazov,* Tolstoy's *War and Peace,* Austen's *Pride and Prejudice,* and Stevenson's compact tale of the Jekyll-Hyde syndrome, far outweigh the forgotten, "factual" nonfiction of the day in those eras.

The dimensional layering is obvious in the convolutions of Marcel Proust or James Joyce, meant to represent inner gestures of consciousness, or in William Faulkner's search for the exact texture of language to represent dissimilar characters in *The Sound and the Fury.* The dimensions are multiplied when the reader enters another person—Jude the Obscure or Jim Burden or Joe Christmas.

A further layering occurs in the cultural and historical milieu readers enter in a novel, unavailable in any other genre, such as the London of Dickens's *Bleak House* or the Russian social fabric of Pushkin's *Eugene Onegin.* Readers are able to experience and measure the events of another time through the eyes and consciousness of another person: the *other.* Readers assume a relationship with this other, who may be the narrator, as in Turgenev's invitation in *Sportsman's Sketches,* "Come, gentle reader, take my hand."[5]

A discerning reader comes to view others with greater understanding and deeper sympathy—a newly enlightened reciprocity. This reader can be humbled to discover the potential of his hidden faults disclosed in a character.

Novels of course contain real facts. I don't believe you'll find a history or biography or even memoir-like journal, such as the one kept by Calaincourt, Napoleon's aide-de-camp, that conveys the brutality of the Napoleonic Wars (or any war), when lines of infantry march into cannon fire as fodder for the motherland with a power comparable to Tolstoy's *War and Peace.* Some of the "facts" are so vivid the reader may never completely recover, or may push up in a chair from a particular novel to find him- or herself an entirely different person.

Here's a fact: the tradition in American fiction is autobiographical, and autobiographical elements exist not only in Herman Melville and Nathaniel Hawthorne but also in Henry James and Mark Twain. A foremost American novelist, one of my favorites, Willa Cather, casts her best work in an autobiographical mould. An American reader can trace the trend as it travels through Sherwood Anderson and John Steinbeck and Eudora Welty to Mary Gordon and Louise Erdrich, but will find its epitome of poetic expression in a pair of earlier writers, F. Scott Fitzgerald and Ernest Hemingway.

Both have their biographers, Matthew Bruccoli and Carlos Baker to begin with, but the biographies don't communicate the substantiality of the facts of their lives as convincingly as their fictions do. All writing is autobiographical in that it rises from a single consciousness, as I remember Saul Bellow once saying, but the best is neither self-centered nor limited to that consciousness. Hemingway had several wives and Fitzgerald had Zelda, a cultic figure visible in a spectrum of Fitzgerald's fiction, most notably as Nicole Diver in *Tender Is the Night*—yet not as she was but a moving metaphor of her in words.

In Hemingway's collection of autobiographical pieces, *A Moveable Feast*, he says Zelda Fitzgerald was zanier than Nicole Diver, and mentions how she came to him once and whispered in a secretive way, "Don't you think Al Jolson is Jesus Christ?"[6]—her grasp of factual reality that dislocated.

Fitzgerald sensed that the aristocrat in America was the person with money, to return to that. And the one with the most money had the potential to wield the greatest power. One side of this is apparent in the Ford and Kennedy and Rockefeller families, all subjects of biographies, and if they are America's aristocrats, we are their courtiers and servants in one or another of the industries or foundations or political consolidations they've established.

Fitzgerald's perception stems from what I think of as the Hem-Fitz dilemma—a puzzle about the uses of power. I first heard about it as a dialogue that scholars used to quote as taking place between Fitzgerald and Hemingway. Fitzgerald is supposed to have said, "The rich are very different from us," to which Hemingway replied, "Yes, they have more money." This is fiction, but the dialogue is so representative of the two it stuck.

The source is a Hemingway story "The Snows of Kilimanjaro," in which a writer dying of gangrene replays his past, and in that inner movie, a metaphor within the metaphor of the story, he mentions another writer, a has-been in his eyes who, he says, viewed the wealthy as "a special glamorous race."[7] Those are the words of the story.

When the first version of "Snows of Kilimanjaro" was published, the has-been writer was called "poor Scott Fitzgerald"—again these are the actual words of the story as it appeared in a magazine. Fitzgerald was of course offended, and wrote a letter to Hemingway asking him to lay off; Fitzgerald was suffering from the "crack-up" he had written about in a series of autobiographical pieces for *Esquire*, but that didn't make him fair game for Hemingway to pile in, too, he said. He graciously asked Hemingway to remove "poor Scott Fitzgerald" from the story when it was collected in a book.

The two were on-again off-again friends for a decade, as comically pictured in Woody Allen's *Midnight in Paris*, and Hemingway, withdrawing from the worst trait that overly sensitive people fall prey to—a bullying destructiveness—complied with Fitzgerald's request. In a postscript to his letter, Fitzgerald added that riches were of no fascination to him "unless accompanied by the greatest charm or distinction."[8] This seems a jab at Hemingway, who at that point in his career was making a lot of money.

When I first heard the version of their exchange, the fictional one that many have heard, I was sure it was true, and imagined Fitzgerald saying the rich were different in order to launch into a sweeping, romantic assessment of the American psyche, all of us Gatsbys, or about the Gerald Murphys, who partly supported Fitzgerald and Hemingway in their expatriate years. I was irritated that Hemingway had the audacity to cut Fitzgerald off, to my imagined sense, by saying, "Right, they have more money."

I wanted to hear Fitzgerald's golden elaboration.

The *fantasy* of what may have happened, or what they might have said, is the reason the *myth* of the conversation persists. I wanted to hear about the rich, who and what they were, but was somewhat smugly satisfied, because I wasn't rich, by the blunt rejoinder: Right, they have more money. Any reader aware of the backgrounds of the two knows that Hemingway held the superior position for actual insight. He was the son of an MD, scion of an upper-middle-class family, and he grew up in a semiposh and sheltered suburb of Chicago, as it was then—Oak Park. His family owned a summer cottage in Michigan where the well-to-do from Chicago were congregating, outside Petoskey, on Walloon Lake.

Fitzgerald was not quite shanty Irish but was an Irish Catholic from Minneapolis, St. Paul, and the opposites in the backgrounds of the two were reversed in their lives. Fitzgerald attended Princeton, at least for a time, and projected the debonair image of old-world aristocracy, while Hemingway, who finished only high school, became a journalist-outdoorsman—opposites teaching two public versions of a way to live.

After WWI, as rebellion and angst entered American expatriates in Paris—the disaffected group Gertrude Stein called "The Lost Generation"—Hemingway and Fitzgerald not only epitomized that generation but found fictional metaphors to depict it. Their attitudes grew into codes of conduct that continue to stand; either we'll have manly grace under pressure (no matter the type) à la Hemingway, or eat, drink, and be merry with Fitzgerald, and perhaps for some fortunate few—the rich?—a bit of both.

If the rich are different from us, it's difficult to measure. "Your mother's cookies don't taste better when you've got a lot of money," the multimillionaire whose biography became a torture to me said, and he experienced riches unknown to either writer. He is a decade younger than both, and lived into the twenty-first century. He was involved most of his life in the macho outdoor world of Hemingway but exhibited the sunny grace that was Fitzgerald's glory when Fitzgerald was young and poor and powerless and entirely unknown.

The genres I've mentioned deal with facts, each in its own manner with methods of its own, because each at its highest level hopes to disclose truth, or in dedicated instances, as in Ralph Ellison's *Invisible Man, the* Truth. Material truth in the world we negotiate has realistic boundaries (I can't walk through that wall) but certain dimensions of truth appear unplumbed. If, for instance, Jesus passed through walls, as he apparently did, should that affect the way I view a wall, not to say the afterlife, in the everyday present? Or perhaps more pertinent: If it does affect my views, can I communicate something of that in words?

It might be possible, but to accomplish that I may have to combine the genres of biography, autobiography, and fiction, along with philosophy and theology, guided by the animating Spirit. To face a final fact, a genre already exists to accommodate all these—the memoir. A way to turn if you've had a hand in every other genre is the memoir, and perhaps that is why so many writers do. Or as Shakespeare says through the metaphor he called Hamlet about the work that occupied him day after day, "*Words, words, words.*" [9]

43

5

USING WORDS,
A CONTINUAL
SPIRITUAL EXERCISE

In *The Varieties of Religious Experience* William James writes: "The science of religions may not be an equivalent for living religion; and if we turn to the inner difficulties of such a science, we see that a point comes when she must drop the purely theoretic attitude, and either let her knots remain uncut, or have them cut by active faith."[1]

James is an apologist for faith, at least partly, and says in his book that faith has the potential to set spiritual goals for humankind. He is equally an apologist for psychology, the science he refers to, although in our day, after exposés of the Freudian slips at the genesis of psychology, I tend to view it as a *creative* science.

Science is anyhow based on faith—that gravity will inhere and maintain the stability for scientific experiment, hold you and your Bunsen burner where you are while you grip a retort or these pages. Science would not have progressed as it has without faith that the universe, from its center to its outermost reaches, does indeed cohere, no matter that the poet W. B. Yeats said "the center cannot hold."[2]

A faith of that sort, assumed and covert, rested beneath *What I'm Going to Do, I Think*, a first novel that appeared in May, 1969, by a writer who signed himself L. Woiwode. The novel was semiscientific and out to cut knots in its detonation of the romantic lie of honeymoons, as it depicted one spent in the Michigan woods not far from Northport Point by Chris and Ellen (Strohe) VanEenanam.

The book received congenial attention, sold well, and started climbing best-seller lists. To sum up the critical reaction, it's fair to say reviewers saw the book as existential and filled with a foreboding they found hard to define. Some mentioned uneasiness at the foreboding and, as the anonymous reviewer from *Time* put it, "After lyrically celebrating the pleasures of love-making, Woiwode begins softly terrorizing paradise."[3]

So paradise was anyway mentioned. One reviewer noted that the first of the three epigraphs, by William Blake, was titled "To God" and read

If you have formed a circle go into
Go into it Yourself and see how You would do.[4]

but none mentioned that the last line of the novel's coda employs a verse from the book of Romans—"The wages of sin, dear, is death." Nor was critical attention turned on the Christian Science that seemed to L. Woiwode to inform his central character, Ellen Strohe, nor the Roman Catholicism of his antagonist, Chris, and Presbyterian and Lutheran outlooks of other characters received no notice, although they often vied with the views of Chris and Ellen.

No reviewer suggested the foreboding might be attributed to belief in an entity beyond the novel, an omniscient Creator, and none implied that the author might believe that a scene in nature (though much was made of his "nature descriptions") could communicate attributes of that Creator—the kind who might cause L. Woiwode and the characters in his novel to assume, one assumes, responsibility for their actions.

Woiwode was born on the Great Plains in 1941 or 1942; both are named by reviewers and websites. The sky and plain seemed to him to govern the universe. They were all he knew until he reached what is perhaps the most critical age—the phase of using words to please parents, and with the use of words he felt suspended between his parents and blue and green, the literal heavens and earth to him.

So his interest in nature and "word pictures," as noted by reviewers of his first novel, was perhaps not merely literary—a correlative to his characters' inner state, as some saw it—but an attempt to represent the heaven and earth containing the lives that contained his from before memory began. And as memory formed, Woiwode felt reluctant to speak, since each word carried a specific meaning.

Would he get it right? An analogue of that reluctance is dramatized by a pair of preschool characters in the novel *Born Brothers*:

> It's difficult for us to fit a word to something it doesn't sound like, especially for him [the narrator's brother]. If the word doesn't match the part of the thing it's meant for, or the thing itself, it slips off the, ah, whatyoumaycallit, you know, that shiny bending thing, wide at the end but flat, for slipping under and lifting—and we learn to use the names that others do, when we do (spatula, for that, for instance, now in Daddy's big hand, turning over eggs crinkled at their edges) out of habit.[5]

Woiwode can't attest to the accuracy of this, once its placement in prose has fixed it in memory as fiction fixes fact, but since both his parents were—in real life, let's say—English teachers, let's imagine they drilled verbal habits into their children.

There was another, higher use of words, however, as Woiwode learned when he was four, in a situation recorded in *Acts*, a memoir-commentary:

> I remember waking (or this is the way the sensation arrives) in church and hearing a priest with a German accent declaim in what seemed anger, in reference to a passage I now know is from First Corinthians, "Does that mean, wives, that you must submit to him when he asks you to go to *bet* wid him? *Yess!*"
>
> With the fervor of his yes! I felt my mother next to me stir in the pew, uneasy, then my father shift on my other side, while I experienced at their center my first faint stirrings of sexual intimation—or

whatever rough secret it was they shared in the bedroom: scripture had been applied.[6]

The decade of 1964 to 1974 was fruitful for L. Woiwode. He wrote portions of every book he has published since, except *Acts*—although he says he was thinking about it, because of his own acts. During this decade he decided to read the Bible to understand what the generations he was writing about found so important.

North Dakota, where his umbilical roots lie (literally, he has said) is the setting of his second novel, *Beyond the Bedroom Wall*. This six-hundred-page book, begun in the mid-sixties and published in 1975 is, if one heeds certain critics, the only book Woiwode has written. Or should be.

Research has shown that other critics felt the novel was inferior to *What I'm Going to Do, I Think*, however, and Woiwode takes heart at that. There was significance in his new *nom de plume*: Larry Woiwode. It wasn't that he was weary of readers responding to portions of his books appearing in magazines with the question, Are you male or female? Or queries on the weirdness of his name—"With all those vowels, I figure you must be East Indian!" His full name did not signal a hope to be wholly straightforward, using the diminutive his parents handed him—though that thought, too, occurred.

What Woiwode hoped to say was, Don't pigeonhole me. The books he was working on tended in different directions, and he noticed how many reviewers and readers, too, clung to the hobgoblin of consistency, preferring books with predictable sameness, so they knew what they were getting into.

In a further sense, perhaps Woiwode reasserted his baptized name to place himself in the centuries-old Christian tradition. The tradition's hallmark is the diversity of its writers. It takes only a glance at moderns in the tradition to appreciate that—John Updike, Muriel Spark, Diane Glancy, or those grounded in the original covenant: Isaac Singer, Cynthia Ozick, Saul Bellow.

Besides the diversity, Woiwode recognized a largesse of spirit in that tradition. A universal understanding of it existed, plus a host of witnesses, which was part of the difficulty in gaining entry. It was that good. Here William James's words on faith fall in place—knots of theory and opposition to be cut. With centuries of scholarship and literary works in its annals, the tradition wasn't one in which you wrote a novel or poem by reinventing the wheel. You stood on or fell from the shoulders of others' achievements, if you stood at all. A sense of the depth and difficulties of the tradition appears in *Beyond the Bedroom Wall*, as Alpha Neumiller considers her entry into the Catholic Church:

> It tied her to a past more ordered than hers. She felt her life lengthen backward, watching rituals she knew had been performed in the same way over the world for hundreds of years happen again; her mind had new strength and freedom to roam now; old fears were given names, others disappeared, and doubts were discarded to gain a new end. The prayers held her in a written framework with her feet on the ground. The Church's scholarship and mysteries were beyond the comprehension of any one man and wife, and she felt an infinity of thought and brotherhood about her.[7]

Couples and *Portnoy's Complaint* and *Fear of Flying* had recently appeared and the title of the novel itself was meant to register transcendence *beyond* bedroom gymnastics. At the end of its first chapter an aging carpenter who has returned to the place of his birth to bury his father reads from a Latin missal and sings Latin hymns in a homemade, graveside rite. The next chapter concludes with the singer's son, Martin, "kneeling in the furnace-heated warmth of St. Boniface Church in Wimbledon, asking God if Alpha could be his wife."[8]

In the next chapter Martin and Alpha study doctrine with a blind priest. The author doesn't sidestep the irony, but doesn't shower a waterfall of condescension down on them, impair them mentally or call them nitwits, as gentle humanists, claiming openness to every aspect of diversity, do.

By now many readers sensed the direction Woiwode's work would take and a number waved good-bye. Others waited. In 1977 he published a book of poems, *Even Tide*, describing the odyssey of a man and woman, and the next year he and his wife moved, with two children (the number would reach four), to southwest North Dakota—the real west, as Woiwode called it.

It was in 1981, with the appearance of his third novel, *Poppa John*, that Woiwode, as ranchers put it, hit the fence. *Poppa John* was generally panned and widely misread—purposely, it sometimes seemed. In the *New York Times Book Review* Joyce Carol Oates claimed Poppa John had a heart attack outside a bank, when in the text a spiritual shakedown occurs *inside* a bank—no clinical heart attack intended or suggested, except by a fellow in the psychiatric ward where Poppa John ends up. Woiwode figured the negative reaction was generated by the novel's bias against America's god: Television.

Trying to set the record straight in an article solicited later by *North Dakota History*, Woiwode noted that he began the book seventeen years earlier—in his fruitful phase as a unisexual East Indian. He mentioned that an editor at the *New Yorker* wanted the magazine to run *Poppa John* entire (not usual in that era), and when the editor was turned down by the man at the top, he lodged an unprecedented request: that Mr. Shawn take two weeks to reconsider. The response that arrived in two weeks gave Woiwode a glimpse of the fence he was about to hit: to publish *Poppa John* might, to some, the top man said, indicate a shift in *New Yorker* policy. The cryptic nature of this Woiwode translated to mean: the magazine could not appear to condone a serious expression of Christianity.

As reviews and reactions to *Poppa John* rolled in, it became clear the novel was seen as an analogue to a "conversion experience" Woiwode must have suffered. He seemed to some not only to leave the high wire of literary performance for a safety net of faith but to set up a pulpit in fiction—a weak-kneed leap of faith?

Another piece of gossip appeared later on the Internet about the paperback edition of *Poppa John*, issued by Crossway—that the Christian house had edited the text to render it acceptable to its audience. They did not touch a word. Woiwode used the opportunity of a new edition to simplify the opening and last pages (running it past his original editor at Farrar, Straus & Giroux first), and Crossway, a true Christian publisher, personified in the Dennis family, reprinted every page of the book as it appeared in the original, including the alterations intended to simplify its opening and conclusion.

OK, I'll slip these suspenders of specious anonymity from my shoulders—I'm the guy!—and say I had not changed, but perhaps my faith became more apparent in that novel. I deplore the idea of a leap of faith. It's irrelevant to Christianity, and is a view of the irrational school of philosophy, as it's called—two of its adherents Kant and Kierkegaard, who tacked flags of philosophy and fiction onto centuries-old biblical texts and commentary.

I don't require a convoluted leap of faith. The Bible contains sixty-plus books and in them I find every shape and shade of belief and unbelief in every form I've experienced (and some I haven't) in translation into clear English. The Word chooses and calls its listeners—"Those with ears to hear, let them hear!"—and they believe and at times fail to believe without the need for philosophical attenuation.

The pages I've composed as a writer, millions of finished sentences, attempt to embody through words aspects of the Word in people and their actions, or to amplify its traditions to include human beings attempting to live out lives of belief or unbelief in the world we all experience daily.

In *Acts* you will find,

> For me, a writer aware of how much more complex each book becomes with each sentence added, it was the clarity of the patterns and structure in Scripture and their ability to intermesh with one another through as many levels as I could imagine that convinced me that the Bible couldn't be the creation of a man or any number of men, and was certainly not the product of separate men divided by centuries, but was of another world: supernatural. I was forced to admit under no pressure but the pressure of the text itself that it could be only what it claimed it was, the Word of God.[9]

This conviction arrived while I was drafting *Beyond the Bedroom*

Wall. In my final work on the novel, I tried to honor that conviction by returning to the Catholic Church I grew up in. But Vatican II had intervened and everything for me was, literally, turned around backward. I didn't feel at home. A year after the novel was published I found what I felt I was looking for in a Presbyterian church. Another tatterdemalion of gossip: that I said this church was better than any other. No, I said a particular church of that denomination seemed right for me at that time in my life. My family and I have since moved to another. A troubling suspicion that's haunted me since is that it seemed OK to be a Catholic—the primary religion of my previous books—as in Walker Percy, J. F. Powers, Flannery O'Connor, Graham Greene, T. S. Eliot and the like, but not a Protestant.

As the quirky response to *Poppa John* kept up, sales of my books slowed. It became harder for my agent to place my work, and Christian reviewers queued up to press the dominant chord, as reviewers do, a few registering their demurrers—unaware, perhaps, how even secondary negativity disrupts the supply of the staff of life. I came to feel approximately the way black citizens felt in America's South in the 1950s—aware my ostracism wasn't that complete, but aggrieved that branches of Christianity added to the apartheid.

And in the isolation booth of self-pity, I thought, Do critics take issue with second raters who climb in the carriage with Camus—the thousands who never contemplate existence with his unflinching originality and dignity? Do they scoff at the self-indulgent sentimentality of nihilism? Or is it only Christians they condemn to hell at the back of the bus?

In my next novel, *Born Brothers*, the narrator says

> I believe in God, the holy catholic church, the communion of saints, and I believe in *history*. The rock that supplied the Israelites with water, and was struck and abused then, is the one that offends to this day. You shepherds are loathsome to Pharaoh, Joseph told his father; that's why he put you out here . . . Israel's tribes kept and milked goats, besides eating them and sheep—lowliest of four-footed animals—but were faithful to other dietary laws that could seem fin-

icky, particularly when they were impoverished . . . and besides this, brought offerings for sacrifice, and gave away a portion of their earnings to a priest or rabbi, and tried to hold to all this, even if the world they traveled through told them they were wrong. Once you've been dismissed as a human being for your beliefs, the next worst form of prejudice . . . is being told you're wrong, often with a shaking finger, and prejudice, whatever form it takes, is a boot in the face.[10]

My "unbelieving" editor did not touch this, perhaps aware that the present prejudice against Christianity is as fervent as ever. More Christians were martyred in the twentieth century than in the previous nineteen added together. Ponder that. Christians are discriminated against by universities and intellectual gatekeepers, even on the daily news, where anybody who takes the Scriptures seriously, whether Baptist or Greek Orthodox or Catholic, is a right-wing fundamentalist. A state religion reigns and its purpose seems to be to banish or at the minimum denigrate Christianity.

I don't believe prayer in public schools is the answer, or even helpful; nor is it proper to expunge references to Christianity from every text, as educators do. This is true censorship, not a group of parents concerned about the content of required reading for a third grader.

You don't have to be a seminarian or law student to understand that Exodus, Leviticus, and Deuteronomy are the basis of common law; that the religious leader Oliver Cromwell enacted the first anti-discrimination laws that opened England to Jews; or that the commandments of the Pentateuch—including prohibitions against murder, slavery, rape, kidnapping, and the abuse of women, to list a few—are the basis of what most of us today consider inviolable human rights.

A relevant sidelight uncovered in the research for a novel, *Indian Affairs* (but does not appear in it) is that the New England Puritans Jonathan Edwards and Cotton Mather worked with Native Americans to transliterate their languages as spoken, as other missionaries did—an irreplaceable addition to the heritage of those nations. The French and British governments involved Indian nations in their internecine, European conflicts, and it wasn't until a commonwealth of states were set up on this continent, and finally a central federal government in-stalled—it was only then that unfair treaties were signed and, one after another, broken.

If Christianity is not allowed fair and free exercise, then the orphan knocking at your door, as Bob Dylan sings, is not only wearing the clothes that you once wore but informing you he isn't your orphan any-more. The stick-figure reject of the media and the target of stale jokes, the person of faith forms the largest homeless segment in the United States—70 percent of the population, strangers and pilgrims here.

As individuals, Christians may tolerate a slap in the face, but as churches and religious organizations it's time to reengage history and occupy the seats at the front of the bus. To encourage that enterprise, they need new stories of the sort they can find in the Bible, which pre-supposes the need for writers, and writing is a spiritual exercise that anybody can join.

You can. Pick up a book. Examine the truth or lack of truth in it; search out the glory of art its creator renders through words. Put off Facebook fads and enter a historic view of Christianity—the basis of day-to-day freedoms—so that political sameness, or newspeak, or whatever we wish to call it, cannot have its perfect work of exclusion and narrow our choices to one. We need to cut a few knots before a cir-cle is formed that we all go into, or the life we once knew will be over for me and for you, Mr. and Mrs. America, and over, too, for the children we hoped to see mature—a threatened and breathless generation going blue in the night, without even the halfway house of William James to settle in for a second wind. No new stories to tell or to listen to.

6

EXAMINING THE WRITER'S IMAGE WITH *IMAGE*

Image: "That Old Dog"[1] is the story of a famous novelist who hasn't written a book in a long time. But over the course of the story, he shows he's capable of learning a few new tricks, and he may have one more great book in him. In some ways it reads like satire but it's also very affecting; we feel for this guy. How closely do you identify with that character? You haven't had the kind of dry spell your character has, but is that sense of the potential for one more great book always with you? That dread of resting on your laurels?

Larry Woiwode: John Updike, in a recent speech from the grave, in his posthumous *Higher Gossip*, says that reviewers tend to compare a writer's later books to earlier ones, generally negatively. And he says that at the beginning a writer is more confident of self and the individual vision he or she enters the fray of publication with. My first two novels received the fullest positive attention, so perhaps Updike is right, and I suspect the encounter with reviewers and critics and editors and readers tends to pollute one's early-on individual vision. As for "That Old Dog," I identify with anybody who's down-and-out and from the start I've particularly identified with older people. The great-grandfather and grandfathers in *Beyond the Bedroom Wall*, for instance, the sitcom actor who has lost his job in *Poppa John*, and the hundred-year-old narrator of my latest novel—not yet out. From my side of the fence, I believe *Born Brothers* is perhaps my best book so far, and by "so far" I of course mean I think the new novel is my best—so, sure, that potential remains. Fifteen years ago I wrote a single sentence, "His status was similar to that of an old dog"—along those lines, and it wasn't until recently that the character who would bear those words stepped up to the plate. It's always risky for a writer to write about a writer, but I hope the comedy and empathy helps the story bounce along.

Image: Your story raises the old question about the relationship between the goodness of the artist and the excellence of the art he or she creates. What's your take on that?

LW: I shy from unresolved brutality, fiction of the sort that begins with somebody being blown away, as in any good detective novel. So I never understood Flannery O'Connor's dictum that to connect in a violent world the writer has to be more violent, since that seems to go against the injunction to turn the other cheek. Her *Mystery and Manners* and *The Habit of Being*, however, are the two best books on writing from a Christian perspective. I would tend to agree with John Gardner who said that most fiction deals with good and evil, so the responsible writer has to take a moral stand. That process is detailed rather exuberantly and sometimes cruelly, as auditors have pointed out, in *On Moral Fiction*. Updike said in response, No, no, no, one must only be honest and accurate (accuracy for Updike was a benchmark); God knows all and is not surprised by anything we write, Updike says in his magnum dicta—as opposed to his magnum opus, the Rabbit Quartet—the autobiography, *Self-Consciousness*. But I believe readers come away from Updike's work surprised or shocked that a person who confesses to be a Christian gets so entangled in graphic sex, while the outpour of his oeuvre can only be classified, from the outside and on the whole, as excellent—particularly his literary reviews and essays on writers and writing. He's the American writer, along with Willa Cather, I nominate for the ages.

Image: Are there fiction writers working now who you particularly admire?

LW: I liked *Matterhorn* by Karl Marlantes a lot—a novel that deals with the war in Vietnam but without ax grinding, neither pro nor con, simply the daily life that soldiers went through there. And Lynn Stegner's *Because a Fire Was in My Head* is wonderful, as her writing usually is, although a dark, dark novel. But I prefer honesty over chrism-varnished Pollyanna people. I'm always interested in what Tom McGuane is up to, and I've followed and liked most of Louise Erdrich's work—shall I say especially the early novels? But also *Tales of Burning Love*. I think a writer whose work takes a clear Christian stand, John Moore, has been underappreciated. I love Tom McGrath and try to keep up with Seamus Heaney.

Image: You once wrote a commentary on the book of Acts, which is surprising from a guy who's mostly known as a fiction writer. How did that come about, and how do you think your background in fiction informed the project? And why *Acts*, instead of some other book of the Bible?

LW: It began with a request to contribute to an anthology on the New Testament. I wanted to write on Ephesians but the editor suggested The Acts of the Apostles, and when I realized it was the longest book in the New Testament I wondered if he wasn't serving justice for my long novels. I did the piece, but it kept hoping to grow and my agent located an editor at HarperSanFrancisco who was interested in a book-length take on Acts, based on the essay. My background in fiction informed the project because Acts is the most narrative book of the New Testament. I also happened to be reading too much theology at the time, and when my editor suggested I incorporate some of my everyday acts in the book, it all fell in place in a pleasant way. Perhaps my tongue is the pen of a too-ready writer.

Image: A collection of your essays came out in 2011, *Words Made Fresh: Essays on Literature and Culture*. What was it like to go back and revisit things you'd written a few years back? Do you find your way of thinking or writing has changed over the years? Do you recognize yourself? What surprised you, if anything?

LW: The essays seemed of a piece and I mostly cut to remove infelicities, where they stood out. With others, such as "Guns," I had the opportunity to bring matters up to the present in a kind of coda. When I began as a writer I used to read everything I wrote to my wife Carole, and her critical acumen, seldom spoken but a powerful magnetic aura, helped train my ear for the times my voice or tone went wrong. After a few years of this an inner person took over and I began to hear my voice from his mouth, as it were, as I wrote, and most of the essays date from that later period, when I was thirty-five or older. It was a pleasure to gather and arrange the essays in a way that made sense to me, and I particularly enjoyed, this time around, the essay on guns, the one on Bob Dylan as mentor of my generation, and those on Updike and Stratford Will—who will forever remain better than anyone anonymous, no matter how many times they rehash those old conspiracy theories about who wrote his plays, Will will.

7

POOLING METAPHORS:
ON WORDS OVERFLOWING

My heart is overflowing with a good theme;
I recite my composition concerning the King;
My tongue is the pen of a ready writer.

Psalm 45:1 NKJV

The heart of an artist's work is metaphor. I'm not sure how to state that with the gravity it deserves. Maybe I should say, *Metaphor is the currency of an artist's economics.* That might convey the weight I want, at the start of this numb decade when most Americans have suffered untraceable shuffling of funds and monetary losses by government entities and borderline gangsters (who seldom go to jail) and are looking for a way out of the morass—economics might convey the proper weight if I say this is the realm artists contend with every day.

Every writer's medium is metaphor. Writers not only work in metaphor and think in it, as they do even away from the keyboard, but the act of writing itself is metaphor. An e-mail you write is a metaphor. The pages of a novel are metaphor. They aren't the thing itself, or life itself, as writers know, and any who don't know that are headed for danger. Metaphors aren't *like* life; that's simile. Metaphors engage with a power greater than simile, or writers wouldn't continue to attend to them.

Finally finished pages aren't the truth itself, quite, though they may reveal elements of it. Truth is too vast for even a collection of books to contain. The proof of this is that writers who matter keep producing more books. A writer of religious inclinations may suspect a single truth, as in "I am the way, and the truth, and the life" or "Sanctify them in the truth; your word is truth."[1] But how does a writer reach that? Truth should rest over and under all that Christians say and do, and especially those who work with words in the hope of fashioning lasting metaphors. But how do words touch or reach the stable of truth?

As a writer works, a sense of those essentials—of this being IT in itself, life itself, like life or better, edging toward actual truth—these shine through the lines of prose or poetry if the writer is good. They register as insight in a writer's pages. It's not that writers are deluded by their immersion in metaphor but gripped by the possibilities that each of those essentials, fixed in metaphor, can lead to.

If not, the work wouldn't affect the reader. Every essential has to engage the writer for a transfer of them into a form similar to, but different from, the essentials themselves. That's a quick definition of metaphor, and it is exactly what writing, the putting of words on paper to designate the otherworld of metaphor, is about.

Samuel Taylor Coleridge had to experience Xanadu in at least an inner sanctum to describe it—before he was, as he said (if we can believe him), so rudely interrupted. But what we have when we pick up his poem is not Xanadu or even Colderidge's view of Xanadu or his internal vision of it, but a transposition of Xanadu into language—the poem printed on a page of a book readers open.[2]

Over the moment of transfer into that other realm every writer, along with Coleridge, is acting on faith, no matter what one's belief or lack of it. And over that moment, Xanadu (or whatever else) better be more real to the writer than the fingers generating the transfer. Fingers better not get in the way any more than the knuckles of poor Porlock about to rap on Coleridge's cerebral door. The writer, a servant of metaphor, as each writer is, cannot be self-absorbed. She can't admire the hair on her forearm more than her metaphor. She better remain so immersed in her metaphor a reader can lean against its buildings and trees.

The form Xanadu is transferred to, as writers understand, is the carefully worked page. Carefully worked, so that the sense of what is being transferred is captured as in a net for as long as the page or poem is read. The net itself is set in place by a studied arrangement of words. The transfer of Xanadu or your essentials—or a *sense* of them—onto a printed page is the process known as metaphor.

Isn't it? I mean, in its largest sense? Because for writers a metaphor is more than a technique or a figurative way of speaking, as in the enduring example from Shakespeare's *As You Like It*—"All the world's a stage."[3] The world, in transposition, is seen as a stage. Men and women are merely actors on the stage, Shakespeare has Jacques say, extending his metaphor.

OK, the world isn't a stage, where people have to beware of splinters in the boards below and avoid a trapdoor, but in ways it is. People have their entrances and exits, births and deaths, and seem participants in a vast, unceasing drama. Or they feel bound in a role whose significance is beyond them, with scenes that sometimes feel ordained, since interrelationships no person could successfully invent occur too often to be called coincidence.

Or the world is the platform on which lives are enacted in a way that causes a few to feel their life is "a walking shadow, a poor player / that struts and frets his hour upon the stage / and then is heard no more"—another metaphor from Shakespeare, as promulgated by the metaphor Macbeth.[4]

In all these instances, an attribute has been transferred to a realm that is different from, but similar to, its usual role: world equals stage, drama equals life (or however you perceive it; we shouldn't enter another's metaphors unless we're asked); and the process by which a description is transferred to an object *by the use of words*, different from yet analogous to its perceived existence, is metaphor.

I'm leaning on the *Oxford English Dictionary* definition, those bones of contention in a suitcase, because metaphor stakes its claim over a writer, and the outlook of his or her work, so entirely it's difficult for a writer to define.

"Time," Vladimir Nabokov writes in *Ada*, "is a fluid medium for the culture of metaphors."[5] By his elegant statement I believe Nabokov means, to be simplistic, that time's ebb and flow in memory is a quick-silver element congenial to setting properly aged metaphors afloat. A metaphor is a sealed message in a bottle, suspended in time's current, present whenever a reader locates it on a page at any period in time. "Time . . . worships language," W. H. Auden says in his elegy for W. B. Yeats;[6] that is, time in its predictable forward progression which we measure by minutes and hours from the day we align with it, merely passes away, while metaphors made of language retain their shape down the centuries, so time is a servant to words and we bow to Shakespeare's magnificent constructions still, bowing to the Word.

In the lyrics to one of his several hundred songs, Bob Dylan says "Time passes slowly when you're lost in a dream."[7]

That's another side to the subject. Dreams that have the artful ability to affect the flow of time, whether daydreams or full-blown visions that appear in sleep or on a page, are metaphors. John Gardner calls fiction the "vivid and continuous dream."[8]

Time is the element linking all of the above to metaphor. Time is the primary element that writing, the making of metaphor, is measured against. The rhythms of language move through time, and timing, including the arrival of the right detail at the exact moment it's needed, is a mark of enduring writing. Hearts tick and thud in iambic progression and time is a dealer of the body's limits—the four-minute mile, the feet per second of rocketry up to the ultimate limit, age and death. Metaphors can age as well as a shapely body or bear up poorly against the passage of time. They can die in a decade or live for centuries—time and time again, time is the ultimate measure.

One sign that an era is over, as others expressed it before Bob Dylan set it into the eloquence of song is, "The times they are *a-changin'*."[9]

I don't believe that when writers sit down to work they automatically think, *How can I make this a workable, enduring metaphor?* It's possible to imagine a proper metaphorical manner for a particular story, though it might be antithetical to the spirit of it, like a prophet thinking, *Now what qualities can I give to God to impress him on my readers?*

That's heresy. But so is the idea that writers work at metaphor in a clinical way, manufacturing meaningful symbols within it. That's an idea advanced by the close reading of literary criticism—or it was before that mannerly form of attention was detonated by deconstruction. It's true that a writer's work arrives in metaphor and his medium is metaphor and metaphor blossoms in the midst of sentences and re-appears as a witness to itself in a crowd of words as surely as, in the medium of soil, a certain host of daffodils.

A novel is merely an extended metaphor, at times a terribly extensive one, such as Tolstoy's *War and Peace*. Or a novel is as surely a metaphor as Randall Jarrell defines it in his wry but appropriate phrase—"a prose narrative of some length that has something wrong with it."[10]

Here's another look at the novel. Imagine an aqua swimming pool and on its surface reflections of leaves of nearby trees, a chain link fence, quivering bricks of a building next door, and telephone wires above all that. Dive in, take the plunge, paddle or stroke the length of it, and when you step out on the other side, the reflections still lie wavering over its surface, unaffected by you, although your senses register the immersion and you're dripping—a kind of quaking mirror picturing the reality of another world. That's metaphor, your swim a dip in a novel.

When a reader enters the mirror of metaphor the reader enters a novel's life.

A novel is as alien from the surround of life as that mirroring pool, in its containment, makeup, displacement, grit, substance—anything you want to reflect on, in whatever way you wish, up to the further truth that metaphor is not the province of writers alone. It is the vehicle of pastors who shepherd a flock—a metaphor that suggests sheep's rebellious one-mindedness and tendency to stray until they're lost. In another context, *Bech: A Book*, John Updike refers to people who deal with lost souls as those "to whom innocence, in its galoshes of rudeness and wet raincoat of presumption, must always appear as an angel possibly to be sheltered and fed."[11] This metaphor is a reminder that writers, working through their metaphors, can confront alarming quirks in characters they believed to be as familiar as members of their family.

Metaphor is also home to philosophers and linguists and mathematicians and scientists and lawyers—all who use symbolic logic. It is the musician's province as surely as the painter's or the filmmaker's or the politician's pedestal. It is employed by teachers and parents and anyone who has to translate the physical world, or elements in it, into terms different from, but mirroring, the original.

Writers' hands are most callused by metaphor, and not from using metaphor in a deliberate manner to impress on readers a mysterious artistry or meanings only a professional can decipher. Any metaphor that is purposely academic or cute bears a stamp of self-congratulation and a writer in that mode is mugging for an audience.

There are exceptions, of course, as in the studied manipulations of Nabokov or Jorge Luis Borges or A. S. Byatt. But they are less exceptions than variations, their manipulations as bruising and real to them, I'm sure, as Studs Lonigan to another, or their work wouldn't engage them and then the reader and carry both breathless to the metaphor's end.

Writers study what *is* and serve as minor experts on that. The key here is "serve." Their best metaphors should represent the world as it exists, and the *IS* may be a rural panorama or the labyrinthine evasions of a character. The writer's duty is to effect a transfer that conveys the essence of the original so that a reader receives the sensation, *This is exactly right; it's inevitable.*

Erik H. Erikson, a philosopher and analyst, noted that "'Reality' is man's most powerful illusion."[12] Nabokov has said that any time we use the word *reality* we should put quotes around it, as Erikson does.

Metaphor must feel as real as the entity being transferred, and in order to fashion reality in its form, so the portrayal is accurately conveyed, the writer has to work within the structure and limitations of language. Unlike others who use metaphor, musicians and visual artists and dancers and potters, a writer is left with one medium and tool—other than his or her sensibilities and a few objects available even to children—language and language alone.

Worse, over the transfer from the original to the page, the writer crosses not only a physical realm—from here to there and this to that; synapses in the brain to a pencil on a page or keys registering images on a computer screen—not only manages that crossing but also crosses a metaphysical impasse where for a moment all that exists is a hope that the springy squiggle of words momentarily held in the cranium will, when they arrive, span the blank abyss of a page. Wordless blankness.

Until that transfer is complete the writer exists wholly on faith.

Before a writer sets down the first words of a poem or book, a metaphor for it has appeared, or the writer has no location to head for. The metaphor might arrive in a tenuous form: a profile, a geometric, a haze of sun-bound blue, a sudden rhythm for which, to echo Igor Stravinsky, all you have to do is find the words. Rhythms assaulted him with such power out of nowhere, as he felt it, or so he relates in *The Poetics of Music*, he knew his job was to compose music to fit the tenuous rhythms' arrivals.

For a novel I was working on, I saw a shape like an hourglass lying on its side. The novel dealt with time, or the overthrow and stilling of time, and I finally realized the shape was a cell in the midst of dividing rather than an hourglass. Then I realized the book had to remain in the wings—*wings!*—until my vision of it cleared. Meanwhile, I had written so many pages, over three hundred, that language, as it registered in my consciousness, had got in the way. I set it aside for two years and after that break away from it, with my inner lens less clouded, *Born Brothers* took off.

Writers not only have to picture a metaphor as it forms but see into it, past potential loopholes, and let it unroll like a length of a cloth or a Chinese scroll. They enter its substance so entirely, as it takes on dimension and detail, that when they look up and see the room around it's a shock. Imagine the times C. S. Lewis had to blink back his study and typewriter keys to keep *Perelandra* intact.

I don't want to seem cavalier when I say writers don't deliberately plan on what their metaphors deliver. That's the perspective of scholars—but where do most writers learn to love reading and *close* reading if not from scholars? A scholar's perspective emphasizes theme and technique and *meaning*, and here's another; for a writer, work in metaphor can amount to a life-and-death matter.

If that seems fatuous, add up the writers who end in suicide, foreign and domestic. The life-and-death dimension to metaphor is as it should be for writers committed to conveying life, and an imperative for those serving one who died for many. In the act of fashioning "reality" in the right form, writers can spend days struggling with their inner sensibilities and the page in a way that feels at the borderline of madness. Sometimes it is. The search for the right word to color a phrase to complete a sentence with the proper weight in order to tip it into the pooling dialogue of metaphor can, at times, tap the writer's last reserves.

Everybody has experienced a similar struggle at times, certainly with temptation, although few struggle to the shedding of blood. At such moments the mind is blanked, as though approaching its personal Armageddon, and the body is a battlefield (as a friend described the experience in an apt metaphor) where good and evil clash. Writers can understand how Faustus sold his soul to Mephistopheles, Christopher Marlowe's metaphor for Satan, in order to get a resistant paragraph to lie down like a good dog on the page.

A false or improper motivation can lead to a crisis as desperate as Faustus's at his end. "See, see, where Christ's blood streams in the firmament!" he cries, able to visualize in his torment attributes of God in the natural world as few have the nerve endings to do. "One drop would save my soul, half a drop. Ah, my Christ!"[13]

What writers face in the most searing revelation is this: I am the God of this creation. That is the original and ultimate fall. It doesn't help that contemporary writing workshops tend to teach young writers that the ultimate attribute, that of creator, can pass one-on-one to *you*—transforming the rankest beginner into a minigod. Seasoned writers recognize the trait and realize they must be metaphorical servants to the work at hand.

The temptation for writers, as with preachers and critics and academics and parents and anybody who deals with others from the cliff face of authority, is to usurp the place of God. He meanwhile, as I experience it, offers aid—the stab of insight, like an inner wound opened, that writers experience in their best moments, rather than a lightning bolt of revelation or lightbulb over the head or waterfall of conclusions illuminating the consciousness, though any of these can occur toward a book or story's close. These momentary insights writers commonly refer to as "inspiration"—not a story or poem arriving intact from the outside, breathed into the brain, as those outside the process and neophytes seem to assume.

Those stabs of momentary insight realign writers—a pool of instant cohesion consolidating the larger metaphor, and I assume Christian writers sense this as the Spirit guiding them toward the goal of bringing every thought into closer conformity to the one who, though he was God, demonstrated that authority best acts as a servant. To understand that is to serve metaphor and your neighbor, too.

But the most dependable servants suffer everyday temptations in transferring truths of the world into the metaphors writing demands. That is, they let work slip, neglect to weave the web as surely as they should, so that what *is*—a housefly of the world, a pest everyone is familiar with, now crawling across the fingers of that character—is not caught with its bulge-eyed hex or luminescent intricacy, the blue-green sheen and shudder of wings that maybe only a prose rhythm can capture. This will take further work, writers have to say.

Further work means discipline and stamina and patience and the constitution of a hod carrier, when metaphors that seem to hold the weight of the world in their weave arrive. To bear that yoke easy is a discipline. It can mean waiting an hour for the right phrase to form rather than pouncing (move too soon and the fly is gone), and yet more patience, as in gradual rewritings the metaphor comes clear.

Metaphor is the meditative center of a writer's inner universe.

To be present in the moment not for the moment but for a broader resolution in the future, a far-off goal, is an emblem of maturity. That maturity cannot be dislodged by current whims or nightly news reports—the culture's dialectical erosion of memory and religion for speeded-up answers provided by the Internet, video games, and the government.

Writers often use or refer to fables or tales or worse, variations on modes of the story as received through other media, including television and film, because they do not trust the internal strands, the complex dimensions, the spiritual implications of their own individual and unique story.

All the lapses I mention are apparent in contemporary fiction, particularly Christian fiction, and I number myself among the transgressors. In *Modern Art and the Death of a Culture*, H. R. Rookmaaker says

> That the Calvinist and Puritan movements (at least from the seventeenth century on) had virtually no appreciation for the fine arts, due to a mystic influence that held that the arts were in themselves worldly, unholy and that a Christian should never participate in them. . . . When the chances did come, much later, in the eighteenth century with the revival of faith with the Wesleys, or with the nineteenth-century revivals, the Protestant stream was no longer interested in the arts at all. . . . Today it is well known that within evangelical Christian circles there is little interest in the arts.[14]

Little effort leads to little interest. Rookmaaker's words appeared in 1970, and it's safe to say the situation hasn't changed, if not gone downhill. His assessment helps account for the modest artistic level of too much Christian writing but also suggests a worse, continuing effect, especially on the young:

> There is no artistic insight, nothing to point to, no answer to the relevant questions of the rising generation. Many want to be artists in a Christian sense—but have to find the answers for themselves. . . . Many have turned away from Christianity or, more tragically, from Christ, as they have come to feel that, if this vital aspect of human life is outside religion or faith, then something basic must be defective in the faith.[15]

I find it hard to believe that fantasy, detached from the actual, can provide answers to the relevant questions of a rising generation. I heard a parent say that children must watch fantasy videos in order to learn to play and develop imagination in their play. No. Fantasy videos limit imagination, containing it inside the boundaries a fantasy imposes— "I'm the Lion King!"—while a child with two rocks and a stick, who has never seen a video, enters truly creative imaginative states. To develop as adults, children have to learn the realities and limits and hard-edged makeup of the physical world, and learn that intellect is a physical force.

Most writers aren't insensitive or blind to intellect or to the metaphors they make or, one imagines, to the effect they may have on others. Good writers gauge that. They hope all will be well. They don't mindlessly blaze ahead, though in some sense they have to, at those moments when they advance on faith. But the metaphor of fiction is not for instilling doctrine, and that's one way that writers of faith, of every stripe, go astray. No reader wants to see a writer step from the wings to the forestage to deliver a sermon on meditation or prayer or a disquisition on Zen or Gandhi or Jesus or, worse, an incumbent political entity or past president. The message is incarnate in the metaphor or it's not.

Once a piece is down, concluded and sealed off in time, the writer begins to recognize it for what it is, and is able to learn from it. Writers are their works' best students—not in a vain but ingenuous manner—and their works' best critics, or had better be, if their writing is going to amount to a hill of beans.

They know their work better than any reader ever will, after months or years inside its metaphor, and as the metaphor reveals itself to them they've learned to follow its lead. This is called rewriting. They highlight portions, blur outlines that appear crayoned in, pare away elements that are peripheral or intrude, with a sense of fashioning their composition into the metaphor it should have been at the start. They try to refine it close to its original feel, rather than create symbols or similes to impress. The page goes stone cold at any premeditated act of self-aggrandizement.

Creative artists work with the specifics of detail rather than the generalities of theme or symbols, and shun premeditated outlines. They picture scenes ahead, or mileposts along the road, rather than numbers of chapters or a series of thesis sentences.

That is the way that writers' minds metaphorically work.

I want to return to that matter of truth, capital T, which Christians believe exists in the body of Scripture and person of Christ. To those looking in from the outside, this might seem a hindrance, an impediment: those armies of unalterable law. But precisely because unvarying truth is unalterable, it holds a writer's feet to the ground as firmly as gravity (whatever that is) and so frees one to follow the complicated turns of the world within the whirlwinds metaphor can incite. Writers must not talk only to those of the enfolded culture, no.

The absolute quality of truth, like the source of it, is infinite, and for every action there is an equal and opposite reaction. Evil gathers where holiness gains. When one employs that elemental equation, drama unfolds, just as the laws of science translate the nature of truth as it exists in the physical world into metaphor. These we call discoveries—Einstein's looping reassessment of linear time.

If one is rooted and grounded in the truth, without having to hold his or her equipment over every element of existence to define it, the outlook should be, ideally, infinite. This is Christian liberty of the highest order. This is the platform for expression and release of a kind readers seldom encounter.

Writers should be giving thanks for that freedom with shoes removed. The earth is holy ground. Our stories and metaphors are a measure of that. Writers should be overflowing with glowing reports on this theme, praising and practicing gifts given, touching on the King—the tongues and pens of writers ready instruments, purged and renewed, printing out treasures in voices infinitely varied yet united by the Spirit. In that spirit writers and readers should be moving into higher expanses of literary standards, of charity, and of yet more praise.

PART TWO

USERS OF WORDS

8

A FIFTY-YEAR WALK
WITH RIGHT WORDS

When I was twelve and what happens to boys hadn't happened to me yet, I loved to walk alone. I would walk five miles down a railroad track to my grandparents' place or walk seven miles in the opposite direction to a lake I liked to look at, after I had walked to the far corners of our town a half dozen times that day. It wasn't beyond me to walk twenty miles without pausing to think about it, as I haven't, really, until now.

The places I liked to walk were outside any sign of habitation—in the carved gap of a railroad line or along a dirt road that led through pastures or cornfields to Mason State Forest, as it was named. When I walked I thought of others who had walked this way before, and about the only ones I had heard of who walked as much as I seemed to walk were the apostles of Jesus (along with Jesus, of course), and a United States president who once lived in the area of Illinois where my family was living, Abraham Lincoln.

The place I liked above all to walk to was Mason State Forest, halfway between my grandparents' and the lake I liked, the straight north of those two points, or so it seemed to me, although its actual direction tended west. I walked toward it along the edge of a road of such pure sand it was as hard to traverse as the sand of a beach. All along the route hedge apples lay in the sand like limes so bloated that the pebbling of their peels looked like worms locked in swollen swirls.

I didn't want to think what they were up to. The hedge apples struck the sand like shot puts and if I kicked one it felt metal heavy and left gooey sap on my bare toes. Hedgerows crowded the road, growing wild in this place as deserted and hot as the Sahara—the perimeter of the forest I was headed toward.

Once I had sized up my route for the next mile, or to the next hill or curve, I never looked ahead of my feet as I walked. I don't know why. What flowed past or flew in from the side or swung up to encounter me was more surprising that way, I suppose. I partly wanted to be surprised, or safely scared, as boys at that age do—a natural scare unable to approach the terror I lived with. My mother was dead and had died away from home of a disease I was never able to fathom and my father never willing to explain, so I had come to feel that my worst thoughts about her had caused her death.

The latticework of shadow from the hedge-apple rows thickened to trunks and the overarching shadow of trees—tall elms free of the Dutch elm blight, burr oaks all gnarled, maples, horse chestnut, and a dozen other varieties our science teacher had pointed out on a field trip when I was so overwhelmed by the trees themselves I could barely remember their names.

But I knew them as well as aunts and uncles from my weekly walks through this forest that was also a wildlife sanctuary. I felt so much at home I sang as I sang nowhere else, sometimes mere notes that touched the tones and patterns of plainsong—this I loved, mingled with incense, as much as anything about the church I attended every Sunday.

"O beautiful trees!" I sang. "O sky above! O *earth* be*neath* my *feet*." It was a shout, blasts of assurance, the same song I sang each time I walked here to announce my presence to the elements I addressed—the earth and sky, green and blue that governed my life from its beginning.

I was never afraid or lost my way no matter how many and how varied the routes I took (besides not looking ahead) and never felt the sense of absence of my mother that I felt everywhere else. She was born on the plains, far from any forest, where an individual tree offered shade but too many got in the way and were a bother to tillage. I had walked with her in the spaces of the plains and at the edges of woods, the blue-green hillsides of Minnesota mostly, and the movement and placement of her limbs as she walked seemed to communicate to me a sense of her ease in either setting. But people were made to talk, unlike the spaces of earth (both empty and filled up) that seemed so inclined to talk they trembled with an omniscience that caused me to listen as I did not with people, not even her.

Now as I sang and walked, matching the words to my right-left pace, I saw rough trunks crowd close, their shadows lying on leaves and needles they shed, their closeness intertwining in a way that caused the light I saw striking my feet to take on substance. The chill of a presence slid over me as if I were shedding leaves and I stopped and looked up. This was the presence of God, I thought, as I watched trees sway and maneuver as if to mount closer to him.

The patterns of the scribbled multitude of twigs and the matching gaps of light corresponding to the movements of their limbs were as much a song as the song I sang. This was the earth, these its trees in their multitude of beauty, twigs to branches to trunks, the sky and space brimming with creatures and murmurs about to break into appearance or speech. I felt no terror, gripped by something of greater substance than my mother's hand, and tears of laughter leaped out like the presences I expected to appear.

One presence was here, I saw, as I turned with my face raised, in the trees and sky and the earth that supported me as I turned. The presence had set all this in place for my pleasure, to teach me about myself and the vibrant present where I stood. I had been instructed to love God but no words I knew in English could approach the language pouring from the forested life with a familiarity that aroused a wordless love I couldn't define.

I was given a glimpse of it when I came to read, *The heavens declare the glory of God . . . day unto day utters speech. . . . There is no speech nor language where their voice is not heard. . . . For since the creation of the world His invisible attributes are clearly seen, being*

understood by the things that are made. . . . For by Him all things were
created that are in heaven and that are on earth, visible and invisible,
whether thrones or principalities or powers. All things were created
through Him and for Him. And He is before all things, and in Him all
things consist.[1]

Here were two languages put into English and what they stated in
the language I was beginning to know was so unimaginable—especially
that last phrase—that I'm jolted from the forest and left flat-footed in
the present.

I studied this statement and found it's so seldom touched on by any
portion of official Christendom you would think it didn't exist. And
the more I studied it and turned it every whichway it still persisted in
saying, *in him all things consist.* How could I reconcile that with my
present-day pragmatic and faint-hearted, tone-deaf view of nature and
my half-numb faith—my hard-heartedness toward grass and trees and
birds and fish and beasts and bracken and oceans and the stormy wind
that fulfills his Word? Lopped off from the boy who hadn't learned to
reason and didn't pay attention to his body and its developments (so
far, anyway) any more than to the developed creation around him, I
seem farther from the truth of the actual words of that statement than
those who worshiped trees and the imaginary or actual spirits trapped
inside them.

And those involved in that worship missed the truth that this statement and the additional ones that I've included appear to teach: it's
much more than trees or the spirits trapped in them, if you see them as
communications of a greater coherence.

Carefully and with the greatest accuracy I may write a description
of my favorite six-foot patch of nature or, if my spirit is feeling expan-
sive, my favorite ten acres, and if anyone who reads it once I'm done
and doesn't sense a hidden attribute of God in the description we are
told is there but try to deny because it doesn't fully fit with the rational-
ism that enlightened thinking (rather than the language of Scripture)
has brought to us, then my description is a failure. Language was given

to return the language the Spirit delivers to those who imagine they hear only when they're plugged into stereophonic ear buds and the like.

On some days, if I lie for hours on the ground or crawl on my belly through grass or weeds or walk in a woods where I might get lost and lie down and take a nap and then wake—on those days I sense voices clamoring from every direction as they did when I was walking in the state forest. How often do I roll in new-mown grass and feel its reek of greenness fill my nostrils until it seems my nose will bleed and realize the reek is the blood of grass, or something more astonishing than my grip on language can deliver?

There are times when, with a warning in my legs of spongy weakness, my body and the earth itself is revealed as molecular—able to give way at any second—and every gesture and word and thought is weighed and measured (right foot, left foot) on shifting scales that are accurate to millimeters of infinity. The earth itself is a handiwork and my treading on it is communicated through a network so complex in its branching even our mightiest computers can't estimate its ultimate effect. I sense this and tend to rest on its evidence even unseen.

This is faith.

In whom do I have faith?

In God.

Where is God?

Everywhere. That's what I learned in the English language.

Then why don't I bump into him or step on him?

I do, in a sense, but wouldn't know if he appeared in front of me, since I so seldom acknowledge that.

If God is everywhere, it's as a spirit. This is the age the Spirit entered this world, and though the world came into being for that purpose, the world does not know or recognize him or receive him or the message the handiwork of this world continues to communicate in details anybody can take in.

A glimpse of the phenomenon was given to a Russian poet suffering the rigors of the Gulag when he tried to read an anthology of modern English poetry with his faulty command of the language. He wrote,

> I remember sitting there in the small wooden shack, peering through the square, porthole-size window at the wet, muddy dirt road with a few stray chickens on it, half believing what I'd just read, half wondering whether my grasp of English wasn't playing tricks on me. I had there a veritable boulder of an English-Russian dictionary, and I went through its pages time and again, checking every word, every allusion, hoping that they might spare me the meaning that stared at me from the page. I guess I was simply refusing to believe that way back in 1939 an English poet had said, "Time. . .worships language," and yet the world around was still what it was.[2]

This is Joseph Brodsky, the Nobel laureate, and he wants readers to understand the effect on him of that distilled statement from Auden's "In Memory of W. B. Yeats"—*time worships language*. Brodsky abhorred delusion and sham and was so attuned to language, and especially the language of the Bible, that he perceived Auden's statement as so stunning it should have altered the world. He went on: "Auden had indeed said that time (not *the* time) worships language, and . . . 'worship' is an attitude of the lesser toward the greater than space."[3]

Language can be turned into omniscient metaphors that form adornments and pool into meaning as long as readers last, while time merely passes away—just as God, through poured-out language, formed worlds that continue to endure. A Russian poet grasped this under straitened conditions but it flies past most with the thrumming beat and glide of a flicker—the bird, I mean, with its yellow-gold ribs and flash of red you can't miss.

When I remember how I drew as if in gulps the words of Brodsky as he explained the struggle he underwent toward his transformation, I see my feet moving through the woods and hear the words of the song I shout more than sing. The words were given to me and just as Brodsky arrived by the labored steps of an unfamiliar language to an understanding that transformed him so that he could not believe the world remained the same, I found agreement in a similar sense. When I wrote, "I feel a pressure behind and turn and there are the cottonwoods and willows at the far end of the street, along the edge of the lake, flying the maidenhair faces of their leaves into the wind, and beyond their crowns of trembling insubstantiality, across the lake dotted with cottonwood pollen, the blue and azure plain abuts against the horizon at infinity"[4]—when I wrote that I knew I would never be the same. It was a period when the balancing scales beneath me were jiggling so much I was sure they would soon give way, and my search became a desire to rest, as though adopting a heavy lean against a tree, on him.

But I forget and become deadened and walk around whispering, Sure, God's everywhere, that's why my life's so wonderful—in a detached and abstract cynicism so bitter it could burn holes in the air. When I had reached a moment like that an age ago, my wife said, "Will you pray, please?" Sure, I thought, sure, I'll pray, and lit into a prayer with such anger a hole indeed seemed to burn through to the presence I'd forgotten or abandoned and I felt the ladder that Jacob had dreamed, with angels ascending and descending on it, appear. The power of the Spirit poured down with such force that prayers for my wife and children, who had gathered, were pressed from me as prayer had never appeared in fifty years, and when I looked up I felt I was seeing each of my family for the first time, transformed.

They were clearly in him, as I was, or they were more than I. They had waited for this confirmation and I had been too cautious and rational and bitter—if I could have explained myself in words—to give in to a worded power mightier than time and I.

I went to bed. It was all I could do. But in bed I couldn't sleep. The pressure that once caused me to turn in recognition exerted a portion of its weight and I couldn't move. I lay underneath that weight, a molecular current overlaying and constraining yet altering me, and every petty act of mine looked like an electron above an abyss in the magnificence of the current flowing through and out of me. I couldn't move for hours. Everyone I had hated or could not forgive appeared over the night, not so I could see them, but I sensed the presence of each and knew who it was and was astonished and grieved at the smallness of my hate in the weighty glory of the forgiveness pouring through me. Tears sprang from my staring eyes as they had in the woods and I was lodged so close to joy I felt that if this was the end, so be it. And it was in a way, perhaps, because I understood I was being called to rise up and walk.

I couldn't move but had to and once I was out of bed and made it from the room, barely—never waking my wife; she never woke the whole night—I ground around the perimeter of two small rooms and a hall, my pacing arena, and got a partial sense of bearing in a body the weight of glory—a few steps all I could bear. I realized I had been prepared for this by that sense of pressure, that turn, but even more by those walks in the woods where I watched my feet lit by the sun as I listened to a language leaping past time and entering in a way I couldn't begin to explain, or would never be able to, I thought, until I sat down and entered that walk on this sunlit afternoon.

9

GETTING WORDS
PLAIN RIGHT TO PUBLISH

For anyone interested in the way writing gets down on a page and published, it's best to listen to those who publish. And now there's a chance
to follow the practice as carried out by a pair of consummate writers.
Their collection of letters, the most intimate and freewheeling form of
writing, gathered in *The Happiness of Getting It Down Right*, allows
readers to follow a duo working together to produce as much good
writing as they are able, in an exchange more engaging than most contemporary novels.[1]

The letters also reveal the relationship between writer and editor
when that relationship is operating as it was intended. This occurs
at least partly because both correspondents are writers (a truth that
doesn't always follow) and one of the two happens to have a half-week
job as editor. Once they begin collaborating on publishable stories and
commenting to each other about them, the pace at which they build on
each other's abilities is, to say the least, instructive.

Family members and other editors occasionally join in the exchange,
but most of the letters are between Frank O'Connor and William Maxwell. O'Connor, protégé of W. B. Yeats and AE (George Russell), was a
notable figure in the Irish literary renaissance kindled by Yeats and Russell. O'Connor was indeed a renaissance man. Self-taught, a translator
of Old Irish and Gaelic, he wrote poetry, short stories, plays, biogra-

phies, autobiographies, memoirs, literary criticism, cultural criticism, history, essays, reviews, and polemics. As he said of himself, "I had always wanted to write poetry, but I realized very early on that I didn't have much talent that way. Story telling is a compensation; the nearest thing one can get to the quality of a pure lyric poem."[2]

At the time of his death in 1966, O'Connor was recognized as one of the foremost Irish writers of the century. The eminent V. S. Pritchett wrote, "It has often been said that Ireland is packed with genius but is short of talent. Frank O'Connor was one of a distinguished generation who had both. His powerful and outspoken voice, above all his moral courage—not a common Irish trait—gave him the air of a thunderous but unbullying Dr. Johnson."[3]

Frank O'Connor was a pseudonym, adopted so that Michael O'Donovan could publish in politically polarized Ireland under its Victorian sensibility. Think of the years of brouhaha and boardroom fuss, for instance, over the publication of Joyce's tame *Dubliners*. As a feisty young man O'Donovan had been imprisoned as an Irish revolutionary, a movement he turned his back on as it became increasingly violent.

So when William Maxwell calls him Michael early in their correspondence, the reader senses what the scrupulous editor of this collection, Michael Steinman, suggests: the closeness of their relationship. Maxwell eventually signs himself "Bill" or merely "B," and O'Connor begins to call him "Willie."

William Maxwell? He is one of the best and brightest but least bruited of contemporary writers—though late in his life he was "discovered" by PBS and Pete Rose and other come-latelies, and now the Library of America series has begun to collect his work, early novels first. He was also an editor at the *New Yorker* for forty years, and during most of that time he spent Monday to Wednesday in his office, busy at his writing the rest of the time. He published six novels, four short-story collections, essays, a memoir, over a dozen books altogether, and his voice, "simultaneously very personal and clairvoyant," as John Updike has noted, "is one of the wisest in American fiction. As well as one of the kindest."[4]

Amen. And he remained wise and personal and clairvoyant and kind after he left his editorial chair, continuing to write into his nineties, including *All the Days and Nights*, collected stories that came out in 1994 from Knopf, one of the better collections of the decade. It is not presumptuous to suggest that Maxwell had as great an influence on the direction of American fiction from the 1940s to the present as any single person—unobtrusively, with no trumpeting or discursive manifestos or self-congratulatory proclamations or publicity seeking.

He first edited poetry at the *New Yorker* but soon came to occupy the post of senior fiction editor—if the designation can be ascribed to anyone in the magazine's formerly loose organization, with everything feeding to the one at the top, first Harold Ross and then William Shawn. During his time at the magazine Maxwell encouraged and edited and helped to raise to its highest level the work not only of O'Connor but also of John O'Hara, Sylvia Townsend Warner, J. D. Salinger, Eudora Welty, John Cheever, Shirley Hazzard, Harold Brodkey, Mavis Gallant, John Updike, and, in his American incarnation, Vladimir Nabokov.

There were literally dozens of others, and a book of correspondence with Maxwell as large as this one, three hundred pages, could be gathered from each of the other dozens—except for Cheever, who regularly burned all letters he received. And if Maxwell had been on hand when Raymond Carver began publishing in the *New Yorker*, Carver might have been a writer he handled, had Maxwell felt OK with the content, because Carver's prose is an unwitting example of the outworking of Maxwell's influence. Keep it simple (within one's personality) and *keep it clear*.

Maxwell's hallmark as a writer was poetic simplicity with an undercurrent of heartrending emotion, as if a plain-spoken Scot had been hot-wired to the mysteries of creation. A common editorial comment, at least to this beneficiary of a decade, was "Isn't there a simpler way of saying it?" Sometimes there wasn't, but often there was. And often, too, while I explained what I wanted in a sentence, he jotted my words on a set of galleys, and said, "That's so much clearer!"

Of course it was. So when O'Connor defines for himself his sense of the story as "a pure lyric poem" it amplifies the excited currency between the two as they work at "the happiness of getting it down right," the title of the book and a phrase of Maxwell's, from an essay in a Knopf festschrift dedicated to O'Connor. That essay, "Frank O'Connor and the *New Yorker*," appears along with comments by family members as an appendix to the letters. It's worth the price of admission alone, for its affectionate portrait of O'Connor and, in a subsidiary sense, a look at "the disease of perfectionism," as Maxwell puts it, that reigned in the heyday of the classic *New Yorker*.[5]

In a letter from 1954, O'Connor writes, "I accept all the admonitions, which, by this time, you must be tired of giving out. As usual on all the minor things which you pick out for correction, you and Lobrano are right. [Gus Lobrano, who first worked with O'Connor, was ill.] You are in immediate relation to the audience."[6]

And Maxwell, who commonly turned letters around the day he received them, responds: "They aren't admonitions, as I'm sure you know, but the illusions of perfectionators, and individually we would probably get tired and quit worrying about this kind of thing, since the story stands or falls elsewhere, but we keep each other at it."[7]

In his introduction to a collection of Sylvia Townsend Warner's letters he edited, Maxwell writes, "The personal correspondence of writers feeds on left-over energy. There is also the element of lavishness, of enjoying the fact that they are throwing away one of their better efforts, for the chances of any given letter's surviving are fifty-fifty, at most. And there is the element of confidence—of the relaxed backhand stroke that can place the ball anywhere in the court that it pleases the writer to have it go."[8]

Letters of that quality abound in this back-and-forth, as when Maxwell whacks a backstroke that emphasizes the colloquial nature of all writing in his compliment to O'Connor on an addition to a story: "We are using the insert, and feel that the use you made of the notebook was a stroke of well why not say genius."[9]

Or this from O'Connor: "I had promised myself lunch with you and Don Congdon [O'Connor's agent] IF I managed to finish the story I was doing for you. It has inspired me to a point when the story is *almost* right but there's still a small knot in the middle which would drive you crazy. Maybe despair will drive me to solve the problem tonight or tomorrow in which case I'll phone you and come."[10]

O'Connor lived for several years in the United States, serving as professor or writing instructor at institutions like Stanford, Northwestern, and Harvard. On one of his first visits to the States he met a student at Harvard, Harriet Rich, and married her; in 1958 they had a daughter and gave her the name Hallie-Og. A few years earlier, Maxwell, then in his forties, and his younger wife Emily had a daughter, Katherine, and another, Brookie, and gradually the letters brim with details of family life. Every writer at some point makes a decision about how he will include his family in his writing, indeed his life, or not include them, and both writers accommodate the demands of their families—a lesson writers (and critics) would do well to contemplate, not dismiss.

To Harriet, for whom Maxwell develops a fondness and addresses when O'Connor is busy or not responding to letters, he writes in June of 1958,

> Kate and Brookie . . . have kept us up between eleven and three or four for three nights running. First Brookie woke up and refused to go back to sleep, so Emmy went to bed in her room, with the window closed, in the kind of general discomfort she contrives for herself when I am not around, out of a belief that comfort isn't everything, and I couldn't get back to sleep because I never can when she is removed from beside me, and so thought about *The New Yorker* all night (TOO MUCH EDITING GOES ON HERE) and what should happen the following night but four violent thunderstorms in succession.[11]

Maxwell as editor was efficient and thorough, sometimes sending off a typed page or two of advice, yet diffident. He set himself aside for the sake of a story. He favored no particular style, as the variety of writers he worked with suggests, but stood for clarity and a simpler way of saying it. Something of his manner of handling details in daily life, was present in his editing; when a decision or conflict faced him, he once told me, his practice was to "wait, silent, with my hands in my pockets," until the matter resolved itself. He generally trusted O'Connor and other writers to solve conflicts in stories and elsewhere themselves, and gave them leeway to do that, while turning away the worst of the checkers' queries with a stroke of a pencil, saying "That's simply nonsense."

He conveys an agreeable, gleeful air, in his delight over everyday details, but can be adamantine, usually when he has to reject a story, perhaps regretting how O'Connor feels and hoping to move to the next submission, as when he writes about stories he's been urging O'Connor to finish: "It is the same as with the last story. The characters do not have the breath of life in them, and so it isn't a story."[12] How awful! If, however, he felt it had the faintest breath, pages of suggestions poured from the rattling upright Royal on his office stand. He explains an element of his nature to O'Connor in this way:

> When I was a very young man, I had to go over a *New Yorker* proof with Edmund Wilson, who snorted from time to time and said in *his* youth he had been an editor on *Vanity Fair*, and that the editorial fallacy was changing things for the sake of changing things. Had I been older, I might have drawn him out, because he is always interesting no matter what he is talking about, but I just took it for a profound and witty remark, which it perhaps was. But *some* editors suffer from the fallacy of guardian angel-ism, and sincerely believe that they are put here on earth to protect authors from damaging their best efforts by after thoughts [*sic.*] that are not an improvement. So I spent three intense, dedicated days going over your two versions of Man of the World, protecting what I feel is one of the most moving and beautiful stories of modern times from your itch to improve it.[13]

O'Connor's reply: "Thanks for your labors on the proofs. I think the results justify the means."[14] The means was, of course, unknown editorial tinkering.

O'Connor's letters, as lyric poet, are often brief, and Maxwell occasionally sends telegrams, as in his initial response to "The Man of the World": "From here it looks very much as if you've earned your way into heaven."[15] He then follows up with a letter in which he says,

> I wondered also if you would know what I was trying to say in the telegram. "This is possibly the best story you have ever written" sounded too much in the accents of posterity, or at least too pleased with my own sense of judgment, but that is how I felt about it. I read it back and forth and around while I was reading it the first time—Do you know that kind of reading, where you circulate among the words and double back to give your feelings time to catch up with you, and for enjoyment. Now he *has* got himself in a pickle, I said, and waited, and openmouthed watched you walk right over the pickle because it wasn't, for your purposes, even there.[16]

Who could resist such clearly stated, levelheaded praise, in the sort of letter every writer hopes to receive?

More than twice the number and bulk of letters are from Maxwell, which is natural, since he is not only editor, but encourager, conscience, gatekeeper, even paymaster. *The New Yorker* rates were so generous it appeared to please him to send off checks, usually accompanied by a note, as this one: "I'm sending, today, a cost of living check to Matson's office [O'Connor's agent] for $1972.35, and thought I'd let you know, in case it might affect your traveling arrangements." And then a concluding backhand stroke: "It is too hot even to go around in your skin."[17]

The magazine's word rate was a dollar or more, and there was also a COLA, the cost-of-living-adjustment Maxwell mentions, based on the rate of inflation and usually issued in quarterly payments—here nearly $2,000 in 1955. And "bonus" payments added increasing percentages of one's total sales for a year to each story over four, then over six, then twelve—a process so lucrative for even the mildly prolific that Maxwell referred to it as "the slot machine."

An added bonus was proffered for signing a yearly contract which stated, in essence, that one would accept such payments. And a few minor perks, such as the black-and-green mottled Venus drawing pencils, perfectly leaded for writing, of a grade of hardness you couldn't get on the street—a luxury item that O'Connor, for one, delighted in pocketing. And lunches with Maxwell at the Century Club, down the street from the *New Yorker* offices. It's no wonder that Nabokov once said in a fictional context, speaking from his experience on several continents, that the *New Yorker* of those days was "the kindest magazine in the world."

Readers will leave these letters with a sense of what it is like to see literary creation rise from the page. A few may be surprised to learn that the relationship of editor to writer, when at its optimum, is never adversarial, as contemporary melodrama tends to depict it. A good editor merely hopes to get the best from a writer, and that was Maxwell's gift—a studied selflessness.

As a writer he understood the difficulty of translating people into the words of a metaphor. And as a writer, or so this collection communicates, he hewed to the traditional literary standard, established by centuries of practice. That is what he keeps turning O'Connor toward. The dizzying middle distance in which the work on a story takes place was a world Maxwell was able to enter, in his clairvoyant way, as easily as the writer, not like a hermit crab, lugging around an ungainly carapace of arbitrariness, but as if inside the writer's skin, the shed metaphor of the story itself. And what he led his writers toward, as much as they were able to follow at the moment, was a standard of excellence where suddenly, when one would least expect it, the standard was all that mattered and the writer was flooded with the happiness of at last getting it down right.

10

TOLSTOY'S WORDS MARCH RIGHT TO TRUTH

In the mid-sixties America and the USSR embarked on a cultural exchange meant to signify a thaw in their relations. The person credited for this was the prime mover behind so much of the reform taking place at the time in American politics, our elegant and aristocratic young president, John F. Kennedy. His counterpart in Russia, Nikita Khrushchev, a stumpy peasant given to banging tables at the United Nations with his shoe, for some reason acceded to the idea.

Yevgeny Yevtushenko and Andrei Voznesenky arrived in New York and began declaiming their poetry from American stages. Our poetic Johns, Cheever and Updike, shy of the Slavic school of declamation, gravely met functionaries and gave readings across the USSR and its iron curtain satellites, as they were called. Vladimir Ashkenazy performed at Carnegie Hall and Kathryn B. Feuer appeared at Yasnaya Polyana, the ancestral estate of Count Lev Nikolayevich Tolstoy.

Feuer, a PhD candidate in 1963, seems an unlikely participant in this stellar constellation, yet the result of her research has an enduring tang. As spotlights beamed on the headliners of the thaw, who were trailed by reporters, Feuer sat in Tolstoy's library, leafing through the handwritten pages of *War and Peace*.

What she was feeling, as her book *Tolstoy and the Genesis of "War and Peace"* conveys in the heat of its prose, is the kind of awe that causes one's knees to give.[1] This emotion can transform the most ordinary mind into an omnivorous trap, and Feuer's mind was by no means ordinary. Her intellect was formidable, scintillating, tending toward the formulaic, and freighted with cool intuition. She was, besides, ironlike in her decisions and formulations, as if she drew the essence of her confidence from Tolstoy's spiky and unwavering hand.

Feuer had originally hoped to write fiction but chose the route that literary hopefuls more commonly choose, graduate study, and never returned to her original love—as similar hopefuls might note. It may be that as she sorted through the four thousand pages that comprise the early drafts of *War and Peace*, she found her ambitions not dashed but fulfilled so presciently she couldn't move from the massed clouds of Tolstoy's mind to creative constructs of her own. We'll never know.

Once she completed her dissertation, she published several articles on Slavic studies, but in the first entry to "Other Works by Kathryn B. Feuer" at the back of *Tolstoy and the Genesis of "War and Peace"*, the reader finds, "*Strike for the Heart,* New York: Doubleday, 1947 (Winner of the Mademoiselle College Fiction Award)"—a novel? a short story?—and realizes she never published another book. Her dissertation of the sixties only recently appeared under the imprint of Cornell Press.

It doesn't seem Feuer was marginalized by the academy's old-boy network. She taught at Berkeley, the University of Virginia, and was for a decade the chair of the Department of Slavic Studies at the University of Toronto. Her trip to Russia, bestowed on a scholar who until then had written primarily fiction, was a plum.

Feuer's editors, her daughter Robin Feuer Miller and Donna Tussing Orwin, both Slavic scholars, are oddly elliptical about her life, as the begetter of these scholars, Tolstoy, would not be, and as Feuer is not in her work. We learn only that Feuer's dissertation, after gaining an underground reputation, was scheduled for publication in the eighties, and that she began rewriting it but never finished before her "untimely death." The date and cause are not disclosed, and you won't find (except perhaps by inference) the institution for which she wrote her dissertation.

Feuer by some trick of imagination is able to enter so entirely Tolstoy's mind the reader participates in his thinking. The rumbling, breathing presence of Tolstoy bulks so eerily in the background, weaving his way through the difficulties of *War and Peace*, it's as if Feuer has added a further character to Tolstoy's already hefty assembly when one rereads the novel. In a sense her Tolstoy is more potent than the Tolstoy of the Tolstoy biographers—Maud, Troyat, Christian, Wilson *et al*—because she has been scrupulous to trace Tolstoy's creative process, following his mind as it moves in loops and backtrackings and seismic bursts of insight as he seeks to find a way, first, simply to begin *War and Peace*.

It wasn't an easy process, as Feuer traces it, but a struggle that lasted five years (not counting Tolstoy's apprentice years, if we may call them that), before he had a glimpse of the book-to-be. In his diary and on manuscript pages he adjures himself, as he had for years, "No digressions!" But the first four openings of *War and Peace* were historical essays, and when he began drafting scenes, he packed them with philosophical or historical or polemical paragraphs, besides commentary on his characters. The truly dramatic element of Feuer's reconstruction of Tolstoy at work is to watch him battle his own worst inclinations and ultimately win.

According to her, *War and Peace* originated in a novel Tolstoy began in 1856, *The Decembrists*, which had risen from a corollary tale, "The Far Field," the idea for which seems to have originated in "The Two Hussars," a long short story. This is how Tolstoy worked as a writer, in interlinked networks of accretion.

When he wrote the autobiographical *Childhood, Boyhood, Youth*, he promised another volume on young manhood, and sometimes claimed *The Cossacks* might be that, and at least once said that it was. But he also bruited *The Cossacks* as the first of a trilogy on military life. In addition he planned a book or series of books on four epochs in the life of a landowner, and some of this transmigrated into the pages he already had, other passages may occur in *Anna Karenina*.

And then history hit home. Tolstoy as a soldier was involved in the

Battle of Sevastopol (1855) and set down his impressions, largely as a reporter, about the Russian defeat—part of the trilogy on military life? In the humiliating aftereffects suffered by the Russian army, he believed a malign foreign influence began entering Russian culture.

Part of the reason was that Tsar Alexander II, in 1856, granted amnesty to the Decembrists, as they were called—a group of Russian military officers who, after a tour of Europe during the reign of Alexander I, experienced the atmosphere of foreign democracies and decided it was time to undo the feudal and Tsarist regime of Russia. They mounted a coup in December of 1825 and failed. Some of the fomenters were executed, some exiled, and others continued in the government, because of the way its bureaucracy worked. Allegiance prevailed only at the top; the rest of the posts filled by flunkies and time-servers, as depicted by writers as early as Nikolai Gogol. When the time came, the government merely changed the pictures on its walls, according to Nabokov, in a manner Gogol foresaw, and the ruling oligarchy called itself Soviet.

But after the defeat at Sevastopol, as if to say something was indeed rotten in Russia, at least in its humbled military, as Tolstoy saw it, the Decembrists were granted amnesty and began returning from exile. Only months earlier, Alexander II called on landowners to cooperate in the emancipation of the serfs "from above rather than to wait until it would begin to abolish itself from below."[2]

To Tolstoy serfdom was a dilemma that Russian landowners had to resolve, a moral stain they could not be cleared of by declarations "from above," or by fiat. Businessmen started organizing the serfs to profit from their release, and this irked Tolstoy, to put it mildly. He was opposed to serfdom but believed he had to work through its inequities with the serfs he had inherited at Yasnaya Polyana. He offered them land at a pittance and they grumbled, expecting it for nothing, because of rumors after the Tsar's declaration. Tolstoy walked away in disgust, set up a school at Yasnaya Polyana, and began to educate the serfs' children.

And in spite of Tolstoy's burn of anger, he granted his serfs freedom.

All this took place in 1856, almost a decade earlier than the Emancipation Proclamation of Abraham Lincoln in the United States. Other situations and influences were at work on Tolstoy, who had recently returned from a European tour himself and was primarily frightened by the workings of democracy he observed. As Feuer traces it through his letters and diaries, he feared for the demise of Russia as he knew it and became, as reductive pop psychology would put it, paranoid.

He was prodded into a creative quest to resolve his fears, in Feuer's eyes, that culminated in *War and Peace*. One need not know the history, which Feuer helps clarify, to appreciate her book. She notes about Tolstoy's manuscripts from the time, they "make it clear that the Decembrist novel plan was still uppermost in his intentions, and that its fundamentally political conception still dominated his thinking. But as the novel grew under his hands it took on a life of its own and began to exert a force that often opposed Tolstoy's thoughts and intentions."[3]

Tolstoy was in Paris in 1857, surveying the ultimate effects of the French Revolution, as he perceived it, and began reading Pierre-Joseph Proudhon and Jean-Jacques Rousseau. He witnessed a guillotine and was so appalled he left Paris—believing he had seen the epitome of barbarism released by the "democracy" of the Revolution. It had produced, ultimately, a despot who seized the crown and placed it on his own head, Napoleon, and as Tolstoy wrote about the advance of Napoleon into Russia in *War and Peace*, he saw in it an analogue to the revolutionary fervor that began entering Russia in 1856, when the Tsar released the Decembrists.

That fervor, he believed, could mean the annihilation of the aristocracy, the class to which he belonged and which, in its independence even from the Tsar, had become the keeper of Russian history and tradition. He mistrusted, even deplored, those who amassed power solely by intellect, such as merchants and monks, and never fairly depicted any in his fiction. He didn't believe people of their stamp could ever experience life in a panoramic manner or understand, for instance, the relationship of serf to land or landowner, much less engage in independent thought. Their intellectuality tended toward theory or took off in the direction of the ruble or got entangled with rubles. This is how Tolstoy saw it and he denigrated their lack of intellectual objectivity. "Tolstoy had accused the liberal emancipators of 'talking trash with a French tongue,'" Feuer notes; and by now he despised everything French.[4]

In his fears for the aristocracy, its annihilation, he was absolutely accurate, only four decades off. And had he seen the revision of history the Soviets practiced, he would have seen his worst nightmares made flesh; after the bodies were carted off, the wisdom of tradition that had been established for centuries was wiped out. The liberal conservatism Tolstoy practiced was akin to the later views of one who hoped to help form a new government once the revolution began, but was forced to flee the country to save his family—V. D. Nabokov, Vladimir Nabokov's father.

The first chapters of the Decembrist novel—all that was completed of it—were incorporated into the early drafts of *War and Peace*, as Feuer ably documents. In its early scenes this novel depicts a weary Decembrist, in return from exile, stopping to visit an aristocrat on his estate—variously called Volkonski or Bolkonski. The aristocrat has served in the government, but in a world-weariness of his own has re-treated to the country. The two discuss politics. This was Tolstoy's route, Feuer, says, to reach contemporaries: "He wrote as an artist for whom one fact—if the right one—was enough, as a moralist distrustful of historians' explanations because they seemed to accept and so justify errors and misfortunes, and as a prophet whose mission was to inspire people, or nations, to salvation's change of heart."[5]

Her view of the politics of the Decembrist novel being carried into *War and Peace* is not entirely original, she admits, but an extension of the discoveries of perhaps the sagest Tolstoy scholar, the early bi-ographer Boris Eikhenbaum. By the time Feuer visited Yasnaya Poly-ana, further careful work on the drafts of *War and Peace* had been accomplished by Evelina Zaidenshnur, so Feuer bore Eikhenbaum's ideas further forward (with added intuitions by the formalist critic Viktor Shklovsky) into what now seems an airtight case: Tolstoy not only brought the political concerns of his Decembrist novel into *War and Peace*; they were the motivation behind it.

But as the novel altered under Tolstoy's hand, one of its least palatable characters became impossible for him to depict. That character split into Anatole Kuragin, and then Pierre Bezukhov, meant to be a revolutionary, rose out of the even-worse original Kuragin's other half. A year later, as Tolstoy started drafting battle scenes in what is known as "The Olmutz-Austerlitz Manuscript," a character on the outlines of Prince Andrei Bolkonsky appeared.

Andrei wasn't at first linked to Natasha, nor was Pierre, until Tolstoy was well underway on later successful drafts of the actual novel. And as the novel changed and grew, it tended in the direction of a novel of social manners, as some say, or a critique of class structure, as Soviet critics were compelled to declare. But a discerning reader will notice the aristocracy is never demeaned.

Feuer is interested in the political genesis of *War and Peace*, she admits, while I'm attuned to the literary accomplishment, the glimpses into techniques that Tolstoy, after his false starts and hesitations, set in place. The scene of revision Feuer quotes most fully, Pierre's visit to his dying father, she uses to illustrate how Tolstoy recognized the power of "limited third-person" point of view, the mastery of which Tolstoy (along with the "interior monologue") was the first to achieve.

War and Peace largely unfolds from an omniscient point of view, but unlike any other nineteenth century novel: in Tolstoy the overseeing consciousness narrows to the confines of the character being presented, so the focus shifts with nearly every scene and sometimes within a scene. Here's how Tolstoy did it. When we look at a first draft of the encounter between Pierre, an illegitimate son, and the father who has never admitted his paternity until his deathbed, we find that Tolstoy first wrote, "How much they had to say to each other, this dying father and his frightened son!" Not much better than a Harlequin Romance or third-rate novel. Then he records the perceptions and physical sensations of each, along with a lot of talk, and finally Pierre takes his father's hand and his father places his other hand on Pierre's head and asks why he hasn't visited him. Pierre bends to his father's face and sobs and says only, "I don't know." Then this: "And on the face of the dying man there appeared a smile expressing the knowledge that there was no need to say anything, that everything was now seen and felt otherwise, that all that was painful, grievous and terrible was over now. They said nothing more."[6] In the final, published draft, Pierre is led into his father's room just as attendants are turning him in his bed and at this moment when the count is being turned over, one of his arms falls back helplessly and he makes a vain effort to move it.

> Either the count noticed the look of terror with which Pierre regarded his lifeless arm or some other idea flashed through his dying mind at that moment, at any rate he looked at the refractory arm, at the expression of terror on Pierre's face, then again at the arm, and on his face there appeared a weak, martyr's smile, a smile that ill accorded with his features, and seemed to make a joke of his own weakness. Unexpectedly, at the sight of this smile, Pierre felt a shuddering in his breast, a pinching sensation in his nose, and tears dimmed his eyes. They turned the sick man on his side, face to the wall. He sighed.[7]

The artistic audacity! And we get only glimpses of the poetic power of the scene, viewing it as we must through a scumbled and muffling medium similar to translucent glass—translation. Here, as in so many portions of *War and Peace*—and in most of Tolstoy's fiction from the 1860s on—the reason for his brilliance is apparent: the psychic gestures of his people, or as a painter might put it, his genius in revealing the "gesture of a pose." More is communicated by the look on the count's face and his flopping arm than by Tolstoy's early two pages of character description.

When Tolstoy realized the effect of gesture and peeled his prose away to reveal each as pure action, he became Tolstoy. The crux of his understanding was this: If I can picture an action as it runs its course or see on a face an exact expression, rather than compose a bagful of prose to explain these, my writing's moving into another realm. The best of that work is pictorial, and he anticipated what would overwhelm our century: first film, then television.

He was blunt and engaging, a philosophical writer, as we can trace, but he forsook all that to get the *look* of a character and the *look* of a scene. He humbled himself and his prose to that rigor—the precise moment a character was passing through—and became a servant to that person within his or her moment. Only genius, coupled with an iron-clad confidence that was perhaps the legacy of his aristocratic up-bringing, is able to stoop to such selflessness.

Tolstoy set aside his forceful, polemic, restless, sifting, contradict-ing intellect for his eye and the emotional repercussions his eye had on his heart. He became his characters' eyes. He is Platon Karataev as surely as Napoleon, and every person in between. He traveled from the dark of his fears down lanes of increasing light that opened onto tracer-ies of brilliance. There he dropped his baggage of books and theories, the privileges of the aristocracy and the rest, and set his plain peasant face toward the end of what we now know as *War and Peace*.

11

NABOKOV'S WORDS
NOT FADING TO NOTHING

Vladimir Nabokov (gnaw-BOAK-uff, as he pronounced his Russian name) is maybe most often invoked by those who never read him as the bad-boy European who wrote that smutty book, *Lolita*. Rather than polish Nabokov's image for the Victorian reader, as aficionados of St. Augustine emphasize his early attraction to heresy and whores to impress the secular reader, it's best to quote from a letter Nabokov wrote to his mother as a young man, in his effort to console her in her continuing decline after her husband's death by assassination:

> Three years have gone—and every trifle relating to father is still as alive as ever inside me. I am so certain, my love, that we will see him again, in an unexpected but completely natural heaven, in a realm where all is radiance and delight. He will come towards us in our common bright eternity, slightly raising his shoulders as he used to do, and we will kiss the birthmark on his hand without surprise. You must live in expectation of that tender hour, my love, and never give in to the temptation of despair. Everything will return.[1]

This was written in Russian in 1925 and still conveys, even in translation, the sweet scent of another century and the affectionate family warmth of earlier Russia, before its language, too, began to be shorn to serve the pragmatics of "dialectical materialism." The extract is from the exhaustively detailed (thirteen hundred pages) and exceptional biography by Brian Boyd, published by Princeton University Press in two volumes in 1990 and 1991—the proper place for anybody who wants to know about the actual person Nabokov to begin. The year Nabokov wrote the letter, he was living in Berlin, in exile, and his mother was trying to scrape together an existence in Czechoslovakia.

His family, of the landed gentry of nineteenth-century Russia, was forced to flee from the rise of Bolshevism. The Rukavishnikovs on his mother's side, some of the largest landowners in Russia, and their many magnificent estates (including one bequeathed to Nabokov when he was twenty-one) had to be left behind—razed or used as quarters for the Red Army. His father, a lawyer and professor, athlete and editor of a progressive newspaper, a liberal who held that change was necessary in Russia, came to abhor and then oppose the chaos of the bloody Marxist revolution.

He was elected to the first provisional parliament formed in Russia, a beacon in Russian history that gave way. He was a hero to some, and when he leaped up to shield a former political enemy who was speaking at a rally in Berlin, he was shot to death by two armed assassins. The intended victim walked away unharmed.

This stuff of myth made up the boyhood and early life of Nabokov. He was born in St. Petersburg in 1899; he attended private school there, the capitol city of Russia at the time, and went to school and back each day in a touring car driven by a liveried chauffeur. Echoes of this mythical past resound through his oeuvre of at least thirty books, depending on your count. The difficulty in tabulation lies in his oeuvre's remarkable, nearly unbelievable nature. Half of it was composed in Russian, the other half in English, with a number of essays and short stories in yet another language, French. To complicate matters, Nabokov, toward the end of his life, translated the Russian and French portions into English and the English into Russian. No such feat has been performed, and certainly not with the artistic élan and accomplishment of Nabokov, in any major body of literature in any century.

Until he was forty-one Nabokov wrote only in Russian, under the pen name of Sirin, while enduring émigré poverty in Berlin and then Paris. But during the years when he was growing up in St. Petersburg or on his family's country estate, his father, an Anglophile, read Dickens to the family, and a governess from England drilled English into the children. There were five; Vladimir was the oldest and cherished by both parents. When he was ready for university he entered Trinity College, Cambridge, and completed a dual major in French and Russian literature—conducted in the apogee of proper English, of course.

So when he saw how awful the translations of his novels from Russian into English were, as measured by his highly attuned literary sensibility, he decided to try to improve one. At the same time, further upheavals in European history, partly related to Communism, by now installed in a country no longer Russia but the Soviet Union, precipitated another flight. Nabokov left Berlin with its brownshirts and Hitlerian brass because of his abhorrence to tyranny, but also for visceral reasons. His wife, the dear and cherished Verá to whom he would remain married until death and to whom he would dedicate every book he wrote, was a Jew.

They hurried first to Paris as the columns of the Third Reich advanced, and Nabokov tried in desperation to find a job or a teaching position in England. Finally, at the last minute, as troops goose-stepped through Paris on their way to the coast, an émigré group in New York, moved by gratitude for the heritage of Nabokov's father, reserved for Vladimir and Verá first-class passage on one of the last liners leaving France for America—torpedoed on its next voyage. Indigent and bedraggled but secure in the sumptuous cabin purchased by Nabokov's father's sacrifice, Nabokov and Verá turned to the prize they'd brought on board, their son Dmitri, lately turned six, who the day before was running such a high fever, of 104 fahrenheit, they didn't believe they would be able to leave.

In the further concatenations of circumstance—a Tolstoyan phrase—this son, their only offspring, translated or helped translate volumes of Nabokov's early work and after Nabokov's death oversaw or edited additions to the Nabokov canon: *The Stories of Vladimir Nabokov, Nabokov's Butterflies, The Original of Laura*, and *The Enchanter*, a precursor to *Lolita* that Nabokov drafted in 1939; and perhaps was working on more, but Dmitri will not himself add further to the oeuvre. He died in 2012.

Over six hundred pages of stories, sixty-five in all, every story Nabokov wanted to preserve (not counting a few lost in that transient existence), his son oversaw, and at least one further story was unearthed by Dmitri after Nabokov's death—the lovely "Sounds," which contains autobiographical elements too telling to allow it to appear at the time it was written, including details later recapitulated in "The Circle," a story detached from Nabokov's final masterpiece in Russian, *Dar*, or *The Gift*, as translated into English by the author. A novel I nominate to take its place beside *The Gift* is *The Luzhin Defense*, besides the academic fumbler who remains in every reader's heart, *Pnin*. The title character of the story "Bachmann" is a precursor to the absently bedazzled chess grandmaster of *The Defense*. Thirteen new stories are gathered in the son-orchestrated collection of Nabokov's stories.

The mythical stuff of which Nabokov's life consisted can be followed through the stories like the thread of life that led to Rahab. But the reader should be cautioned not to expect autobiographical snippets. It is the shape and exhilaration and poetic power of the stories that convey not only Nabokov's mythical past but also the repercussions of his loss of the past.

In an early story, a young artist, a sculptor (his methods and studio are scrupulously described) is waiting near the Brandenburg Gate for a last meeting with a woman he loves, even though he is convinced she will not appear. He begins to notice a stout street person, like the homeless of contemporary America, trying to sell tattered postcards from her seat on the sidewalk, to no avail. A soldier in the guardhouse at the gate offers her a cup of coffee, and the narrator watches her consume it with relish in the cold fall air:

Here I became aware of the world's tenderness, the profound beneficence of all that surrounded me, the blissful bond between me and
all of creation, and I realized that the joy I had sought in you [the
woman he hoped to meet] was not only secreted in you, but breathed
around me everywhere, in the speeding street sounds, in the hem of a
comically lifted skirt, in the metallic yet tender drone of the wind, in
the autumn clouds bloated with rain. I realized that the world does
not represent a struggle at all, or a predaceous sequence of chance
events, but shimmering bliss, beneficent trepidation, a gift bestowed
on us and unappreciated.[2]

The young sculptor, stunned by the gift of life itself, is transported
to the other side of loss, and appreciates the unappreciated bestowal. In
the beauty of creation, the lovely complexity of the natural world itself,
Nabokov, who was a lepidopterist of renown and worked at Harvard's
Museum of Comparative Zoology, was able to pass beyond the material manifestations of his near-fictional past and delight in an existence
that was not "a predaceous sequence of chance events."

Few writers who claim Christian appreciation for the world's surround have conveyed its beauty with Nabokov's poetic verve.

The short story may not be the most difficult form to manage
(though it gets my vote), but it's the genre in which it's least easy to
hide your dirty socks, as it were. A writer has to enter a story with the
heady momentum of a poet going whole hog in the hope a poem's final
line will contain *all* and meanwhile fashion each sentence so the reader
is able to follow from the end of one into the next without the least
slip from its metaphor to the story's inevitable end (as it should feel),
its final sentence. That sentence should set off a buzzer or send your
head bumping up through the story's length to its *first* sentence; or as
Nabokov says, cause the tip of the spine to tingle, the only indisputable
sign, to him, of real writing.

Anybody who composes a few dozen ordered and contained
constructions called stories—"the shapes a bright container can contain!"[3]—no matter how hard that writer hopes to avoid personality
pitfalls that reveal the shameful monster beneath, the writer in the end

stands exposed. So maybe it's relevant that Nabokov began with poetry and moved to the short story and then to the novel.

He never tried to palliate an audience, or play up to or, worse, down to one, and his observations and conclusions open the reader's mind to possibilities in new and memorable modes, as in "La Veneziana," an early story of family deceptions and transmutations caused by a forged masterpiece:

> How radiantly the world's monotony is interrupted now and then by the book of a genius, a comet, a crime, or even simply a single sleepless night. Our laws, though—our pulse, our digestion are firmly linked to the harmonious motion of the stars, and any attempt to disturb this regularity is punished, at worst by beheading, at best by a headache. Then again, the world was unquestionably created with good intentions.[4]

Or this description of the city where an émigré presently lives, written to a young woman he once loved and had to leave in St. Petersburg:

> A car rolls by on pillars of wet light. It is black, with a yellow stripe beneath the windows. It trumpets gruffly into the ear of the night, and its shadow passes under my feet. By now the street is totally deserted—except for an aged Great Dane whose claws rap on the sidewalk as it reluctantly takes for a walk a listless, pretty, hatless girl with an opened umbrella. When she passes under the garnet bulb (on her left, above the fire alarm), a single taut, black segment of her umbrella reddens damply.[5]

The perhaps easy pathos of this story's title, "A Letter That Never Reached Russia," looms over its unfolding like the reddening segment of the umbrella, but its author was only twenty-five, as he was when he wrote the letter of comfort, one of many, to his mother; and in the final sentence the reader glimpses Nabokov's mature self: "The centuries will roll by, and schoolboys will yawn over the history of our upheavals; everything will pass, but my happiness, dear, my happiness will remain, in the moist reflection of a streetlamp, in the cautious bend of stone steps that descend into the canal's black waters, in the smiles of a dancing couple, in everything with which God so generously surrounds human loneliness."[6]

Now that Nabokov's life is over and increasingly chronicled, one can see that this "Letter" was equally addressed to his mother and to Mother Russia, his first undimmed loves. A year later, as Boyd's biography illuminates when consulted in conjunction with the stories, the young Nabokov began to formulate his artistic aesthetic. In a series of postmodern vignettes entitled "A Guide To Berlin," the narrator steps forward in a postmodern manner and states,

> I think that here lies the sense of literary creation: to portray ordinary objects as they will be reflected in the kindly mirrors of future times; to find in the objects around us the fragrant tenderness that only posterity will discern and appreciate in the far-off times when every trifle of our plain everyday life will become exquisite and festive in its own right: the times when a man who might put on the most ordinary jacket of today will be dressed up for an elegant masquerade.[7]

How did this gentle and elegant aristocrat come to write lurid *Lolita*? Part of the answer, of course, is that Lolita and Humbert and Quilty had predecessors, and in the American version are dressed up in dowdy sinfulness, as each passing year suggests, for a masquerade that will prove elegant or otherwise. It was also Nabokov's practice to invert his personality, or dramatize the opposite of a cherished belief, or to oppose aspects of himself, as when Shakespeare pits Iago against Othello, in order to gather readers to sanity's side.

Those who knew Nabokov have remarked that his affection for Dmitri was extraordinary, even excessive; and perhaps Nabokov, sensing that, employed a pre-pubescent girl in order to examine his over-zealousness, hedged with caution (think NAMBLA), in this disturbing novel that ultimately conveys moral gravity. In a larger sense, I believe that Nabokov, who toured across America more widely than most Americans, from coast to coast and north to south—often in a search of a specific species of butterfly—came to embrace his adopted country so completely he wrote a horribly graphic and macabre parable of how

America's youth is being stained by the polymorphic sins of a decaying old world, including latter-day infusions of Marxism. It was in Europe that Nabokov and Verá, with Dmitri, endured what must have felt like personal apocalypse, twice.

It is a surprise to learn from Nabokov's notes to this collection (often taken from previous collections) that he wrote only nine stories in English, not counting "First Love."[8] This grew into an early chapter of his autobiography, *Speak, Memory*. Short stories are indeed difficult, and although Nabokov brought to every piece of prose a chiseled precision that heirs as diverse as John Updike and Thomas Pynchon yearned to imitate, he never quite mastered the comfortable yet compressed music in English that a story demands, as he had orchestrated it so well in Russian—more a project anyway for the stout nerves of one-minded youth. With age the brain heads off on excursions unimaginable to youth. In 1951, when Nabokov was fifty-two, it appears he banished any hope in that resistant genre and moved to novels after the nightmarish session he endured to complete his last story, "Lance."

During the work on "Lance," sentences and phrases assaulted him with a harrowing immediacy that kept him awake for days; he stalked in circles dazed and shaking, and later said the story was an attempt to assuage his fears about Dmitri. His son had taken to mountaineering on America's most precipitous cliff faces and peaks. It's a curious story—bare minimum. On its surface it seems involved in space travel, decades before any county's forays into space (remember Russia was first), but it's also about mountaineering and an arresting climb toward death:

> The classical ex-mortal leans on his elbow from a flowered ledge to contemplate the earth, this toy, this teetotum gyrating on slow display in its model firmament, every feature so gay and clear—the painted oceans, and the praying woman of the Baltic, and a still of the elegant Americas caught in their trapeze act, and Australia like a baby Africa lying on its side. There may be people among my coevals who half expect their spirits to look down from Heaven with a shudder and a sigh at their native planet and see it girdled with latitudes, stayed

with meridians, and marked, perhaps, with the fat, black, diabolically curving arrows of global wars.[9]

The narrator understands how the "young descendant on his first night out, in the imagined silence of an unimaginable world, would have to view the surface features of our globe through the depths of its atmosphere"—this long before any photos were relayed from outer space—which "would mean dust, scattered reflections, haze, and all kinds of optical pitfalls, so that continents, if they appeared at all through the varying clouds, would slip by in queer disguises, with inexplicable gleams of color and unrecognizable outlines. But this is a minor point. The problem is: Will the mind of the explorer survive the shock?"[10] Nabokov is broaching here, as he often does in his fiction, the possibility, in various conditions, of an existence after death. More than any writer of the twentieth century, perhaps, Nabokov reached for and brought back intimations of an otherworld that coexisted with the same-old we take for granted. He believed in that world with a sturdy aloofness that put people off, as many are put off by his mere mention of heaven, as a growing multitude is put off by any mention of a spiritual otherworld.

From the time of the letter to his mother Nabokov anticipated that world, at times with trepidation but mostly with the arch and tender metaphors he conveys in his prose. In one of his later novels in English, which even his ingrained detractors—from whichever camp—acknowledge as a minor masterpiece on the lines of a tour de force, *Pale Fire*, Nabokov puts into the mouth of one of his most untrustworthy narrators, the unruly Kinbote, a portion of the credo Nabokov kept scattering through interviews near the end of his life:

> As St. Augustine said, "One can know what God is not; one cannot know what He is." I think I know what he is not: He is not despair, He is not terror, He is not the earth in one's rattling throat, not the black hum in one's ears fading to nothing in nothing. I know also that the world could not have occurred fortuitously and that somehow Mind is involved as a main factor in the making of the universe. In trying to find the right name for that Universal Mind, or First Cause, or the Absolute, or Nature, I submit that the name of God has priority.[11]

12

EXCHANGING WORDS: AURAL NORTHERN LIGHTS

"You say you're working on something about childhood."

"Children."

"You make a distinction?"

"The ideas people have about childhood run along the lines of an innocent state, an irresponsible one, or the time parents repress you. The way people look at childhood is distorted by memory, tied to cuteness or whimsy. Neither is my favorite mode."

"But your work is about childhood."

"About a relationship that begins when two brothers are children. It moves on from there but their beginning is the basis of the rest. I agree with Freud, for reasons other than his, that the first five years are the most important."

"What about adulthood and decision making?"

"People who avoid secondhand opinions or the pressures that start in school and allow the world to imprint itself on them have the foundation of a true child."

"But that's gone in a blink, at our age."

"If we could enter that time we might find parts we want to claim rather than feel it's baggage we're carrying around. That period is us with no frills."

"For most it exists in a kind of merciful amnesia."

"As a doctor, you might think that, and I don't doubt that many people believe that and hope that others do, too."

"What do you mean, *hope*?"

"The idea is so appealing! It confirms we're mature! It's how we'd live if our senses didn't suggest something other—not to mention those who end on a psychiatrist's couch. I mean the past's power to teach, warn, and heal."

"Heal?"

"You're a psychiatrist."

"Sort of."

"A doctor whose practice is—what did you say?—seventy percent shrinking. I think 'shrinking' was your word."

"OK, integration of personality."

"The route to that is, *If I can get my thinking out in words, I'm integrated*. Children have a sense of that from the start: *words are power*. They try to match words to their experience of the world at the same time they're caught in its ongoing open-endedness. You can say the experience is like a movie, but movies are images a camera records that have little depth without language. With a film like *The Artist* my internal word processor supplies meaning to facial expressions and the rest."

"I don't see how that relates to childhood—sorry, children."

"They're the best potential storytellers! They take in phenomena they haven't categorized and name it their way. Everything is new to them, with references in every direction. When I try to recapture that state, I can't say whether it was partly visual or verbal in its mad rush or even more astonishing. A child has no boundaries or self-regard—the sophisticated sides of being verbal—and when a child sees an ocean for the first time he can only cry, *Ahh!*—no language for it."

"You must imagine there's some appeal to this."

"If our senses weren't deadened by the media, which is opposed to actual perception, we might take in the world differently. Media mediates it. The difference is comparable to standing in the Grand Canyon and trying to take it in through your dwarfed consciousness, in its *threat* to you, or looking at a photograph that sets you outside it. That's the media."

"I would tend to think *language* gets in the way."

"That is a problem. But language, when worked with, can register the immensity with the least intrusion. It's the everyday currency even children—"

"But you said—"

"—the everyday medium available to children that's wide-ranging enough to take in the Grand Canyon. It's everything in that diction-ary . . . No, the unabridged one, there—everything in it, from cover to cover, is free for the taking."

"This isn't merely important to you—"

"It keeps me occupied. And in a metaphor of words I live in sweeps of experience unlike anything else. It would be a shame not to let you in on that."

"That's what you want to do?"

"Assume our first years form a grid at our base—different for each of us but there. If we could project it on a screen we'd see tapestry so complex it would be beyond the skill of human hands. We'd go '*Ahh!*' like the boy seeing the ocean. We can't reverse the grid or discover what this *thing*, once set in place, seals off. We incline or dive toward defini-tions. We have breakdowns or daydream hours away. People drink or use drugs to try to hammer their way out."

"I have no idea where you're going with this."

"Is the cosmos as organized as science finds it? Do we ignore an overseeing other-than-human source? In Psalm 139, the 'I' says his *frame* wasn't hidden 'when I was being made in secret, intricately woven in the depths of the earth.' His unformed substance, he says, was *seen*, and 'in your book were written, every one of them, the days that were formed for me, when as yet there were none of them.'"[1]

"That's a psalm!"

"An astonishing thought, wherever it's from. I'm not saying that's the answer but it's a clue to where I'm going. I get a sense of that in déjà vu—that this has happened in exactly this way, under these identical circumstances, once before. Déjà vu gives a glimpse of the other side. Science trusts or moves ahead on faith; it insists on the composition and reaction and weight of this or that, because the planet itself coheres. So when I sense an incident has happened this way before, I'm getting a glimpse of the incident as it originated at the same second I experience it. Maybe it was 'written in a book,' too, before it arrived."

"That's unbelievable."

"Why, when a lowly computer can do as much?"

"I don't think so."

"Run a business from monthly billing to assembly line, foresee stock market trends, and whip a chess master—all in one day?—and computers are products of human hands. Déjà vu may seem eerie but never harms. It leads to steps into the past—the integration you mentioned—and is interesting enough so we think, even on the laziest level, *Hmmm*. The connections are right at the fringe."

"How about a simple act of fate, as Bob Dylan calls it?"

"Fate threatens. Déjà vu sets a space around the moment so we're cushioned from everything else to focus on *it*—a thread in the tapestry. You may suffer a sense of seeing double as the moment has its hold on you, but you emerge with a clear mind, thinking *Hmm,* if only I could make exact connections!"

"You sound like a mystic."

"A mystic's freedom is personal choice. Mine is the opposite."

"I'm not sure I get that."

"I'm an ecological superrealist."

"Run that past me again."

"I sense my place in a tangible order and keep in touch with it. I have a family. I garden and farm and keep track of horses and birds and wildlife."

"You said the farm doesn't support you."

"You might say the projects support my spirits so I'm able to stay on the farm. Most farming today is marginal, doubly so on a small farm."

"What farm—sorry—what *form* do you see your metaphor taking?"

"I don't know."

"You don't know."

"If it fell from me the way 'You don't know' fell from you, I'd be assured I had the right words. A combination of enough of them tends to dictate its form."

"Surely you have some plan—an idea of a style, at least, or a technique!"

"I work three to eight hours a day, six days a week. Sometimes I pray. You smile. That's my technique. About style I'd say most efforts to produce style are useless. 'Develop a style,' you hear. How about 'Develop a bustline'? You can, maybe, if you've got one—that grid."

"You mean the 'grid' that matches the one in me, both of which match another, which might be infinite?"

"Maybe, minus the irony. Everything from my first memory to the last is built on my 'formative years'—an acceptable definition. I don't deny that everybody's individual, but in a broader sense we're microcosms, we have commonalities, we're members of the human race. New ways of responding to experience arrive with experience itself—filigree builds across the grid, although we can't alter the events that formed it. We're hardly conscious it's there until we age. Here, let me shut the recorder off and we'll take a break."

"If I were to take what you've said as gospel, I'd be tempted to say you believe environment shapes us."

"It adds dimension to a shape already present—the rare individuality parents recognize in a newborn. You begin to go your own way, too, but come against limits—the *No* you hear from them, often for your own good. I mean parents. After a while life has the feel of variations. We can squander adulthood in puzzlement if we're not aware of that."

"I imagine some might view this as heady, for a farmer."

"Prejudice is comic in the way it protrudes. And considering how many have gone back to the land, as it's put, we might be entering a new Jeffersonian era—every intellectual and political strategist a farmer. No, let me finish. Farmers may seem slow at times, as when they're interrupted by a stranger asking, 'Where am I?' And if they seem slow it's because they're attuned to the timing of whatever they raise within the cycle of nature. They have to be intelligent to establish order over all the variables of a farm."

"Don't you find your work boring?"

"Boredom is fear. If not fear of the situation in front of us or fear of how we'd have to change ourselves to take part in it, then fear of what we might have to do to create an alternative. It's a sophisticated version of the reflex of backing from a threat—walking out on a lousy concert, for instance, even though we're front row center. But to be afraid is not intellectually acceptable. So every intellectual and every pretender-to-be is *bored*."

"The first five years seem intellectual to you?"

"I stretch the limits, yes. But it's certain we'll learn something at our beginnings and not our end. Those who take that exit haven't reported back."

"I can't relate this to children."

"'The child is father of the man.'[2] It's not that you can't take the boy out of the man, as people may think Wordsworth was saying—that isn't what he's saying, and the idea grates on me, too. Such a boy, as man, doesn't have a hold on who he is or he wouldn't act like an adolescent. We have plenty of those. Rather, the child exists before the adult and discovers the world firsthand. The experience might be limited, but perceptions arrive as they won't, quite, later."

"He or she won't learn anything from then on?"

"Not to the same depth."

"So environment does have an effect."

"If that's how you see it, imagine an organization having an effect before we enter the environment. Is a newborn's brain mush or what's in those convolutions?"

"It's a wise child?"

"Wise in the way of manipulating parents, maybe, from knowledge passed on in the genes from each. Look at the way a younger child uses wordless cries or facial expressions to incite an older one to wildness."

"Words work better."

"So much better the older one is provoked to strike out, as he shouldn't."

"I get it."

"There has to be a level of understanding they enter, trickier than the one we're operating in now, for that to happen."

"Observation coupled with perversity."

"Why can't we observe like them, then, perverse or not, and have the same effect? They operate out of a realm our intellect can't penetrate."

"Why not say children are primitive, since they don't handle adult concepts?"

"If you're saying the child existed in a certain way, primitive as you put it, before the adult, that's better than Wordsworth—better than denying a child's existence or saying they know nothing until they get to sex."

"Sex!"

"Sex has no limits for a child, as with another person or below the belt, and if you view adolescence as other than a phase to get through, you're likely to end up a perpetual, grown-up adolescent."

"A necessary phase of growth."

"Barely mentioned till the twentieth century. Dickens wrote about young adults. Adolescence seems a creation of psychology—"

"I doubt that."

"Too many in their twenties and thirties aren't over it yet, living in a parent's basement, ready to join any noisy gang that foments rebellion—where anything that gets in the way of one's right to entire freedom is unbearably frustrating!"

"You're real one-minded about this."

"How does that go? 'I'm tenacious, she's one-minded, you're pig-headed, he's perverse'? Consider the adolescent fun that's seldom fun and lately deadly. Even if you eliminate the parents, they remain in your memory—those last looks."

"Are you setting up your preference for a society of children?"

"My preference is for a healthy adult who is measured in thought

117

and action, conflicts resolved. Every child has a pair of adults guiding it, for better or worse, or that's the way it was for generations, one on each hand for life."

"What if undeveloped children in adults are leading the child?"

"That's what I hope would change, and it's the marriage of all of them, a trio of accord, that's best. Children take in what they're told and want to know right and wrong, why this is the way it is, and expect advice if they're off base."

"Pretty perfect little creatures."

"That's a caricature, kitsch, a porcelain angel—and not *tabulae rasae* either. Their appreciation of mystery hasn't been dulled by logic or taken the plunge into rebellion, followed by irony, so their nerves are wide open—receptors of darker forces, too. They need steadfast parents like you."

"Me?"

"When your son asks a question, it's not because he doesn't know what's going on—he may see into it in ways you don't—but he wants your interpretation. That's teaching. Everything you say defines his existence, and if you try to narrow him to a cutout based on your pattern, he'll rebel. Children ultimately settle at the feet of their parents, and whether that's fortunate or not is up to you."

"Once they're grown up."

"In this grown-up era."

"With grown-up responsibilities."

"True."

"Your ongoing skeptic would have to say we've almost agreed. What is it, really, you're working on? Tell me."

"It deals with a pair of brothers a year apart in age—a mathematical reason why their first years are important; they won't spend much time together again."

"Why not admit one of the brothers is you."

"If that helps. What I hope to get at is the inevitability of our relationship and how it continues in ways it's impossible to predict, even though you were in it from the start. The bond is nearly chemical or *is* chemical in the strictest sense, when you enumerate genes and the rest. We were like twins."

"In a way, with you elevated to my level."

"I wasn't quite grasping your heel when I arrived, but we were that close."

"You're referring to Jacob and Esau—*bad* example."

"You were always looking back at me and I was looking forward, and we've kept our separate directions. I'm headed to a future that's your past and you seem to be going back to when you were the only beloved of our parents. You've always had an abstract look, as if seeing through me, although I'm sitting right here."

"Beloved?"

"They were affectionate, maybe more so with only one, and you were the first. Their presences are the light and shadow that define us, and we met each other on middle ground with our separate dispositions, in a light that seems to run through us from another source, uniting us before birth. It can't be traced except by picking up the strand at our start. That's what I'm trying to do."

"In this amorphous adulthood without a defining grid?"

"Our identities do spill into each other's as they probably wouldn't if our parents had lived longer—she was gone at thirty-four, Dad at sixty-two—or if they'd existed in their original strength. Maybe we dimmed that."

"Maybe we did."

"I want to see if the maybes can be removed. The place was important, North Dakota, with its northern lights like boundaries of a frontier. What a world and what a way of life that was and what a way to see it in its first light, pristine!"

"Can you?"

"If I can get the details under that light, maybe it's possible. From this distance, the light looks like rain from a higher atmosphere, though it's hard to judge the height of rain from below. In that light I may be able to separate myself from you and head for what's to come. It's a matter of life and death."

"Don't get desperate again."

"I mean everyday physical concerns. How we existed, the way you wore a cap, how its angle could anger me—you a year ahead. If we resemble Jacob and Esau, we were also like Cain and Abel."

"True. Deadly."

"Brotherhood is my theme, within the changes since WWII in city and rural life. That war, with its international communication, was the turning point in our time. I want to be able to pass in and out of that era and for that to happen the years have to continue to exist. I didn't have any words for it then and I don't now."

"Please."

"Aspects of 'please,' of memory's source and power, yes, and the way a shared perspective can fashion a single outlook."

"That's quite an order."

"I'll have help. I also want to convey how it feels to be recording, at the age I am, the end of a time—in the mere instance of not hearing jet noise, or false cracks of thunder from jets, in the sky back then—merely on that level."

"Help, you say?"

"You, in the way you've already helped, yes."

"I have?"

"You'll be the central character."

"I was afraid of that."

"Beyond the character you are right now. It's time to put my words into practice and pull our separate selves in place. There. How does that feel?"

"About the same."

"So you're comfortable with this."

"I didn't say that. Wait a minute. Goodness, *now* I see! Now I know why you want to let that light in and why you keep talking about children, not childhood!"

"Fine, but it's late and I'm ready for bed."

"On, no, let's get on with this!"

"Here. Let's pause at the window. What do you see?"

"Northern lights!"

"What? I didn't realize they were out. It's the latitude. We're so close to the aural zone we see them sometimes all summer—solar eruptions you hardly notice unless they're spectacular. The force of them affecting me feels doubled! You know what?"

"Don't define it. I'm with you there, too."

"You are?"

"This has happened before, in exactly this way, as you said about déjà vu."

"Shall we enter the next development together?"

"We better."

"We're here, mirrored in a window the northern lights shine through. A brotherhood in the form of a single face. See? Testing, testing, five, four, three . . ."

13

WITH *INSIDE'S* WORDS INSIDE SUNY ACADEMY

Inside:[1] I find it extraordinary that you've supported yourself and your family by freelance writing. Most serious writers are attached to universities. How have you managed? Did you have a hidden source of wealth?

Larry Woiwode: Approximately the opposite, so no. It's been manageable as long as the *New Yorker* takes a piece now and then. They offer a first reading agreement to writers who once were, or are, regular contributors. This establishes a certain word-payment rate and after the sale of so many stories a quantity bonus kicks in. If you're selling regularly there, you can make a living. Cheever and O'Hara and Beattie and others have. Novels became another source of income. I've had the advances from novels stretched out to two or three years. I used to get foreign translations but not many lately. The anthology appearances and so forth, as Updike wittily mentions in *Bech: A Book*, usually amount to $87.22, depending on how much it's nibbled at. Regular sales at the *New Yorker* made the difference.

Inside: I suspect that's why *Beyond the Bedroom Wall* first appeared as short stories.

LW: About a third did. Publication in a magazine or journal is a first serial right, as it's called, and after publication the ownership reverts to the writer who holds the copyright. It's then available to sell to whomever wants it whenever they do—for an anthology, say. Some critics noted that portions of the book appeared as stories, and maybe because they didn't consider the economics of surviving as a writer, the sequence mystified them.

Inside: But the sequence was a way to get double mileage, so to speak, out of the work. Right?

LW: I was able to work on only certain sections of *Bedroom Wall* at the time. Once I had some sense of what the book would amount to, I knew I couldn't dive in and draft it straight through, which is my preferred way to do it. So I worked on parts of it at a stretch. If a piece seemed to work as a story, fine, I fixed it up that way and sent it off. When I put the book together, though, the stories became something other, one thirteen-pager now over sixty, another ten-pager doubled. The only pieces that remain fairly much as they appeared in the *New Yorker* are in the opening sections. I don't see the sequence gaining quite the mileage a professor gets for the same lecture notes year after year.

Inside: Did you always intend to be a freelancer?

LW: A writer. I wasn't sure how it would work out. When I was done with college, I worked for a while for a television station, and then decided to try to write what I wanted to, and gave myself a year in New York for that.

Inside: What kind of TV work?

LW: Mostly writing advertising and trailer copy for a CBS affiliate.

Inside: So you know what it's like to be a nine-to-fiver after all.

LW: Oh, yes, and writing is more like seven to twelve. There have been spells when I've felt if only I could go to a job from eight to five and have it over with, be free of my entanglements with these people, the characters, free of getting words down from the time I wake till I fall asleep, how nice that would be! I know many workers bring their jobs home, but perhaps not in quite such a visceral way.

Inside: You mentioned going to New York. Why did you feel that was necessary?

LW: New York is the publishing Zion, isn't it? Most magazines and publishing houses and agents are there. It's the center, it seems, for the arts, and I was primed at that age for the excitement this implied. I wanted to make as many connections as I could. I was invited to visit an editor who knew about my fiction. If you expect to be a writer and have published or hope to, it's probably best to go to the city and work out relationships with editors and agents—the people you might be beholden to the rest of your life—in person.

Inside: You didn't see a need to remain there?

LW: Once the relationships were established, no—unless you find the literary ambience so exciting you can't leave. But the literary politics can be a drain on energy put to better use. Hemingway compared the internal politics of New York to a jar of tapeworms.

Inside: Given your success at freelancing, why did you decide to come to SUNY-Binghamton?

LW: I was invited right after the death of John Gardner. My view is that a writer should write, as the title implies. On the other hand, I'd been sitting on the plains a few years, on a farm we knew couldn't support us, though we had hoped it would pay its mortgage. It didn't. My writing pretty much took care of things until *Poppa John*. After that, it was tough. When the offer came, I thought, No, I should stay, because we were beginning to get settled in as a family. But the more my wife and I talked about it, the more we came to agree now was the time.

I like working with young writers, and there's a sense in which I feel I should pass on what I've learned. I had been doing two-day, three-day, and ten-day workshops—which is how I preferred it. But this was something other. I felt perhaps I could carry on with the kind of program Gardner had established without retailoring it to my personal whims.

But speaking about it in this way limits its complexity, or the effect of his death on me. My daughter came running out one afternoon to the office where I work with the news that he was dead. She'd heard it on the radio. Maybe it has something to say about my growing sense of mortality, but I don't think I've been so grieved by the death of a writer. And I hardly knew him. We talked once. It was after he had reviewed *Bedroom Wall*. He heard I was going to be close to where he was teaching and said he wanted to meet me. When I walked in he said to his wife, "See, I told you he wasn't as dumb-looking as that *Times* picture made him seem." I think we both got too tipsy to say anything of literary interest. But a couple of months before my daughter came running out I had reviewed his *Mickelsson's Ghosts* and had felt, well, his *presence*, and not only that but fear for his well-being, reading portions of him into Mickelsson's straits.

And there's another side. My wife and I were concerned about our children's education and wanted to teach them at home, at least over their first years. We learned this was illegal in my home state. That wasn't in accord with the Federal Constitution, we thought, and ended up having the state drag us through its court system for a year. It was an awful drain on our time, our finances, our spirits, and depressing to find that in the state where my great-grandparents homesteaded, a basic freedom was denied us. Our families had emigrated here, her grandparents from Norway, for precisely such freedoms. So the impetus to be out of that atmosphere grew stronger in the spring when, though we thought we were done with this, the state came after us again. So I called the chair of the English Department who originally offered the appointment and he said they had already filled the position—this was with Galway Kinnell—but wanted me to interview anyway, so here I am.

Inside: Do you still own the farm?

LW: So far. We plan to be back this summer. My relationship to SUNY at the moment is, as they say, up in the air. When I arrived, we had a mutual agreement to try this for a year. That's what I requested. But things have worked out better than anybody expected—or perhaps better than I had.

Inside: So you would like to stay?

LW: At first I said I didn't think it was time to take a full-time teaching job, which has been my stock answer for years. Now I don't know.

Inside: Your formal education is not very extensive.

LW: Four years of college. I switched curriculum so many times I never got credits enough for a major. I've published books and have a doctorate I feel I've earned. I did research for years and wrote and rewrote for a decade to put together a six-hundred page book. That's only one of them.

Inside: The people we call our "serious writers," aren't they usually professors or people with graduate educations? Aren't you somewhat unusual in this respect?

LW: It's a recent attitude, and mostly in the academy, that writers should have degrees. Hemingway and Faulkner didn't continue past high school. Fitzgerald went to Princeton but lasted only a semester, or maybe it was a year. The best education for a writer is working under the tutelage of another writer or an exceptional editor. I happen to have had the best of both worlds, by the grace of God, working at the side of William Maxwell. To step back a bit, Tolstoy never finished college, nor did another favorite writer, Colette. Dostoyevsky received a degree, I believe, but in engineering. Then there's Melville. A degree was rushed to Samuel Johnson, after he politicked for it, as his dictionary was coming out, so he could add LLD to the title page. That strangely pained mad bear never made it through Oxford.

I was intimidated by Gardner's suitcase of degrees, I admit, and then learned his PhD wasn't in medieval literature. Both his advanced degrees were in creative writing. I bring an edge, I think, as a working novelist, one who's made a living at this for a number of years. Gardner probably could have supported himself with his writing, anyway after *Grendel*, but for whatever reasons he was always with a college or university. A formal education can be helpful to a writer—I'm grateful for my years at the University of Illinois—but the structure a university must maintain simply to function, can paralyze a writer. Writers can't run with the crowd.

Inside: Do you suppose this could have something to do with the reason why so many people with university educations, who have been exposed to good literature, don't read a word of it after they graduate?

LW: It's possible. I understand half of university graduates read one book a year, *if*. Reading can be made to seem a chore if too much emphasis is put on symbol and theme and hidden meaning, which only the prof knows, when it should be a joy. At least a *minimum* of joy should be involved.

Inside: It seems to be that deciding what good literature is—that's a definition we get from the universities. The critics themselves are academics who write criticism as a sideline.

LW: That's good, a good insight. Their criticism is a sideline—they don't live by it. But try to engage one with the idea that university professors don't control the canon, even one who *doesn't* write! I think there would be a difference in their judgments, if not writing in general, if their work were the sole means by which they earned their bread.

They wouldn't make sweeping statements about novels and writers, I suspect, or would tend to tread more carefully, because they would now understand those are lives they're treading on. My children have to eat.

Inside: That's not considered.

LW: I don't know that the novel asked the university to define it. The university assumed that responsibility, because it was the place where classics were once read. At the end of the nineteenth century, English literature was imported into British universities, largely to raise the level of the working class, as it was seen, but also because religion was dying. People needed a new "belief system," as it's put, and at that point the academy took over the canon and became its high priests. Critics like Johnson and Coleridge and De Quincey had written about writers past and present as another means of earning their way. They were working writers, not professors, and sometimes they encouraged fellow workers, or tried to purge scribblers from their field. Even Poe did interesting criticism when he wasn't inventing how he wrote "The Raven" after he wrote it. If I have a place in the academy, it's not as a critical theorist, but a worker in words with a sense of how a novel works. I can give quick advice to young writers that will save them a lot of time.

Inside: You have done criticism yourself.

LW: What I've done is usually from inside the process itself. I don't think of what I write as superseding the text I examine, as many modern critics do.

Inside: But you wouldn't be reluctant to cut somebody down if you felt they had written a bad book.

LW: I'll gladly identify schlock, but think I should resist cutting down a *body*, a person, *ad hominem*. I've asked for passes on books sent to me for review if I felt an aversion to them, for whatever reason. Let somebody who likes the book write about it, or one who gets a thrill from literary homicide. Writers who aren't working toward a position in the AWP [the Association of Writing Programs] have to say at times something is awful—they're the last outpost. The quality of criticism in the *New York Times Book Review* and daily *Times* seems to have dimmed. When Stephen King can be mentioned in the *Times* in the same breath as Henry James, by saying King's "otherwise masterly" *Pet Semetary* has a minor flaw in point of view, as defined in a James preface, a certain sense of distinction seems to have slipped.

Inside: How does your interest in farming and being out in the country and working with your hands tie in to being a writer?

LW: Without farmers, we'd have no food, we'd die, and that's a helpful daily reminder. Books can be helpful, too, saving us from personal trauma by means of a vicarious metaphor that teaches and warns. But if you're at a desk or keyboard having to get out so many words a day, you can get stuck. So I go out and ride a horse or a piece of machinery or walk around to check how a crop is doing, and my mind is freed. Words appear and I'm part of the world again, encouraged to write.

Inside: What are your writing habits like?

LW: I work about four hours a day drafting. I think that's all the real creative time any writer has. Then there are proofs and correspondence and working on past drafts and the rest. Four or five handwritten pages of draft a day is my goal. Updike set his at three, which was enough to see pages add up, he's said, but not so unreachable it was a discouragement. I tend to do several drafts. I used to do dozens but seem to have learned with age.

Inside: You haven't been swept up in the word processing mania?

LW: No. I've been experimenting with a computer at SUNY, and it's interesting to see how easily one can manipulate a page. But to stare at a screen instead of paper is an alien sensation to me. That's an *image* of a word on the screen, not a real word, and there's something distancing about it that I'm not sure isn't antithetical to the way I work. I can't compose on a computer yet. I get headaches.

Inside: What about the market for fiction these days? What do you tell your serious students?

LW: That the prospects are pretty bleak, and unless you feel called to be a writer, better look elsewhere. Right now fewer than a hundred writers in the United States make a living writing fiction. If you include those who write romance or pulp, narrow it. That's the way it is. For some reason, either due to the kind of criticism grounded in the university, or to television, the sensibility for fiction seems to be fading. In one of my first graduate seminars we talked about the improbability of making a living at this—unless of course you're a committed writer whose work takes off. In a certain respect the academy has been a refuge. It's supported wonderful writers like Roethke. At its best it can operate like a king's court, or as the church used to—a patron that makes it possible for apprentices to work with a professional.

Inside: Have you ever abandoned any work?

LW: All the time. Other work I've set aside because I don't know where it's going or I'm not ready for it yet. *Poppa John* was idling for seventeen years before I was able to get it down and out. The novel I'm working on now has been around for twenty. There's a novel I believe I've entirely abandoned, but I might use pieces of it somehow. I'm acquainted with false starts and I have files of poetry and short stories that didn't come off.

Inside: What are some of the consequences of becoming a literary celebrity?

LW: I'm not sure I am, though lately I seem to sit for a lot of interviews. Apparently writers are supposed to issue pronouncements, as many do, usually on politics, when almost everything I want to say I've tried to say with precision in a book. I've spent most of my life trying to get words in proper order on a page.

Inside: What are some of the other consequences of success?

LW: To be truly successful, a writer should go on a publicity tour, or that's the wisdom, to the talk shows on radio and TV, so I guess I'm not. Life in that lane can be destructive. A writer should write. Leave the promotion to people who get paid for it. When a writer finishes a novel, that's usually about all of consequence there is to say until the next one.

Inside: What does it do for one's ego, for example, to be regarded as part of the literary establishment?

LW: I don't think I am. I believe I'm viewed as being on a retreat from that establishment. I left New York not so much to flee it as for solitude. Like every writer, the most important work I do is in isolation. To get out in public or to give a reading, to enact my fiction, which is essentially what one does at a reading, is to move to the opposite pole from writing. You become a performer and any performance sets a shield over your inner self.

Inside: Do you have any interest in writing for more popular media such as television or film?

LW: No.

Inside: Why?

LW: They're floundering for a definition of what they are—especially television. I don't want my work caught in that or all control taken from me, as Hollywood does.

Inside: What are your goals? Do you have expectations that your best work is ahead of you?

LW: My best work is, I think, in a stack on my desk at home right now. It's the book *Bedroom Wall* rose from, about the relationship in a family, especially between two brothers, over a period of thirty years.

Inside: From time to time, do you find yourself involuntarily thinking about your place among other writers, making comparisons?

LW: It's best not to compare, I tell students. Each person is unique, incomparable. We can't be compared to others if writing rises from an innate individuality. I feel irritants at times at the edges of what I'm doing, yes. There are misunderstandings about my writing and that isn't comfortable. But for the last ten years I've pretty much known where I stand and what I'm doing and where I'm going.

14

WORDS AT THE LAST FROM A MARTYR WHO LIVES

Two months before Aleksandr Men was felled with an ax, an interviewer asked him on a radio program broadcast across Russia, "Does one need to be a Christian, and if one does, then why?"

"I think there is only one answer and it is as follows," Men said to the question that seems a gotcha no matter the continent, with a dozen paths to go down. "Man always seeks God. The normal state of man is, to some extent, to be connected with a higher power, even when the higher power in the human mind is distorted, and turned into something secular. Still, eras of Stalinism, Moldesuism, and all other isms seek some false god even if God is taken away. This turns to idol worship, but still the inner instinct of seeking God is there."

Imagine Men in a Soviet-style studio, drawing closer to the microphone as he continues to ad lib his answer on the spot, "The question is totally different when it is put this way: Why Christianity? Is it because of the sacred scriptures? No, every religion has sacred scriptures, and sometimes with a very high quality of spiritual content . . .

"Then why Christianity? Morality? Certainly. I am happy that in our society high moral values of Christianity are accepted, but it would be totally erroneous to maintain that there are no moral values outside Christianity . . .

"Then why Christianity? Should we embrace pluralism of religion;

or should we embrace a position that God is revealed and therefore can be found in any kind of religion? No, because then the uniqueness and absolute character of Christianity will disappear.

"I think that nothing will prove the uniqueness of Christianity except one thing—Jesus Christ himself."

In the reflex of an Orthodox priest at the name of Jesus, Men perhaps placed his right hand—fingers like a concert pianist's—across the crucifix suspended over his chest, below his gray-streaked beard. "Many religious teachers, I am sure, have a degree of truth in what they preach, but let's listen to them: Buddha said that he could reach the state of absolute nothingness only after long and hard exercise. Can we believe him? We can. He is a good man. He reached what he worked hard for. Greek philosophers tell us how difficult it is for the mind to reach the idea of God and the truth. Mohammed says he felt miserable before God. He felt like nobody, but God simply revealed himself to him. Mohammed was like a little fly before God. Can we believe him? Yes.

"Among these religious teachers there is only one who says, 'And I say to you,' as if he is speaking on behalf of God." Imagine Men's fingers curling around the crucifix in a gesture that sets his Semitic face in relief. "As the Gospel of John would say 'I and the Father are one.' Among the great teachers of world religions, nobody ever said anything like that. This is the only instance in history when God so fully revealed himself through a man—Jesus Christ, the God-man.

"It is a historical myth that Jesus simply preached morals. He could not be crucified for just doing that. Someone might say, 'He called himself Messiah.' Yes, but Berkeley also called himself messiah, and he was not crucified for that. There were many false messiahs. Why was he so loved and hated? He said, 'I am the door'—the door into eternity.

"I believe that everything that is of value in Christianity is valuable only because it belongs to Christ. If it doesn't belong to Christ, it belongs to the same degree to Islam or Buddhism. So every religion is an attempt to reach God. But Jesus Christ is the only answer."

The Moscow State Radio interviewer probably nearly tipped in his chair but Men quietly continued, saying, "On one hand he is the framework of history. On the other he is totally unique. Christianity is unique because Christ is unique."[1]

That was his answer, pared down, under the pressure of an interview that the KGB was listening in on, as Men knew. And that was only the opening. Men spoke with the same alert eloquence for another half hour. It was July 19, 1990, and the disassembly of the Soviet system was nearly complete, or so consumers of United States television and newsweeklies were taught to believe.

Before *glasnost* and *perestroika* were bywords on the nightly news, Aleksandr Men was a beacon of reform across the Soviet Union. In his modest church in a Moscow suburb, where intelligentsia flocked, even unlettered workers understood his sermons and lecture presentations of the gospel. Part of the teaching of the Bible is that particular gifts are bestowed on believers, but the honed clarity Men exemplified does not drop from the stars.[2]

He was born in Moscow in 1935. Both parents were Jews. His father, an engineer, was an official atheist and nonpracticing Jew, but sympathetic to the Jewish community. In the early 1930s, during a period of bloody anti-Christian purges, Men's mother Elena met Fr. Serafim Batukov, a priest in the catacomb, the Russian underground church. As a child Elena was a seeker, and as a young woman active in the Zionist movement. Now she received Fr. Serafim's teachings.

Seven months after her first son, Alik, was born, Elena took him in secret to Fr. Serafim's house in Zagorsk.[3] There she and Alik were baptized together. She joined Fr. Serafim's community and moved to Zagorsk. Seven years later, as the elderly priest lay dying, he said to Elena, "Thanks to what you are enduring and to the serious way you are raising him, your Alik will someday be a great man."

Young Alik Men, who was nurtured by Fr. Serafim until the priest's death, turned to Boris Vasilev, a scientist and theologian and member of Serafim's church. At the age of thirteen, Men rapped on the door of the Moscow Theological Seminary, located in Zagorsk, and asked to be admitted. He was turned down, but the dean of students was so impressed by Men's abilities—he had begun to master Latin, Greek, and Hebrew as well as several modern European languages—he became Men's lifelong confidant.

Men's younger brother, Pavel, an Orthodox believer who later taught Hebrew in Moscow, says Men felt called to the ministry at the age of twelve. "He sought out religious literature wherever he could find it. I can still see him in a Moscow market, poring over books by great religious philosophers. 'They inoculated me against the pestilence of Stalin,' he once told me. 'I trembled as I read.'"

When he was fourteen, Men began writing a life of Christ. Within the year he finished a first draft—a book that eventually became volume one in a series on the history of world religions. Men loved the natural world and in an effort to know it better studied biology—first in Moscow, then at Irkutsk, in Siberia. He later said that because of his training under Vasilev he never sensed a contradiction between faith and science.

His roommate at Irkutsk was Gleb Yakunin, a biology student and an atheist. Men persuaded Yakunin to rejoin the Russian Orthodox Church, where he had been baptized, and Yakunin was later ordained a priest and became a defender of human rights in the Soviet Union. After the overthrow of communism, Yakunin became a deputy in the Duma, the lower house of Russia's parliament.

The year Men should have received his degree in biology he was expelled from the institute as "a practicing church member." Because of his earlier call to the gospel he entered the seminary at Zagorsk, and his call was confirmed, for him, when Israel became a nation in 1948. If Jesus was the Messiah of Israel, as he taught, the people of Israel would eventually acknowledge that, Men felt, and once they did and were gathered from diaspora into a national identity, he believed they would study what he called their "Jewish legacy—the New Testament." The need for Jewish preachers of the gospel then, he was convinced, would be momentous.

In 1958 he married, and on the feast of Pentecost that summer he was ordained a deacon—two years later ordained a priest. He served parishes close to Moscow, but only as an assistant. Higher-ups disliked the popularity of his ministry. Worship services, previously attended mostly by elderly women, began to swell with crowds attracted by his preaching. Men baptized the songwriter Aleksandr Galich, the memoirist and cultural commentator Nadhezda Mandelstam (widow of the Russian poet, Osip Mandelstam, who died in a Soviet labor camp in 1938), and the writer Andrei Sinyavsky—later condemned to seven years in the Gulag. Men was spiritual advisor to Alexander Solzhenitsyn and the Nobel Prize-winning physicist Andrei Sakharov.

Parishioners and friends perceived him as joyous, a source of rare discernment; he seemed to sense spiritual needs and convey to others the love of Christ—a light-hearted spiritual healer. In nearly every photograph he is smiling or conveys the unclouded look of a person whose joy rises straight from the heart.

He read all he could, his memory apparently encyclopedic. He wrote a six-volume history of religious and philosophical thought in the Eastern and Western cultures before the appearance of Christ—beginning with the volume he drafted when he was fourteen, *Syn chelovecheskii*, his life of Christ. The series ended with the New Testament teachings of Christ extending into the world. That work, according to his biographer, Yves Hamant, exceeds four thousand pages. In addition to another encyclopedic work, a seven-volume dictionary of biblical studies, Men wrote books and essays on Orthodox worship and on how to read the Bible—a true need in tradition-fogged, officially atheist Soviet Russia.

The vibrancy of Jesus as revealed in the gospels, Men felt, would reanimate the thousand-year-old Orthodox Church—aware that its Russian branch underwent compromises with the Soviet regime simply to exist. His books, circulated in samizdat, loosened the Soviet claim of atheism as a science and championed Christ as the truly intellectual way. These writings convey the appealing person of Christ, according to Michael Meerson, and brought about change in the Orthodox Church.

Thousands of young people were converted by them. Men's popularity aroused the ire of not only the government but also of clerics in the established church. The hierarchy moved him from Moscow to the small parish of Novaya Derevnya.

Michael Meerson visited Men there, at the house where he lived for twenty years.

> I found him working in his garden, watering plants. He was reading a book held in his left hand, reciting something to himself, while watering with his right hand. "What are you reciting, Father," I asked him. "Dante's *Divine Comedy*," he replied. "I cannot live without it, I know it almost by heart, and reread it several times a year to keep it in my memory." . . . Conversation with him was an intellectual feast: his language was picturesque, full of puns, literary allusions, and quotations from memory, of poetry of the mystical literature of East and West, and of Scriptures, which he knew brilliantly.[4]

Certain of the hierarchy in the Orthodox Church hoped to suppress Men—denouncing him in the church and in public to the Soviet authorities and the press. Those authorities, who had shadowed Men for years, moved in. For six years the KGB kept him under surveillance, and during 1985 and 1986 subjected him to searches and seizures and harassment. He was compelled to meet with the KGB several times a week. They threatened him with deportation and prison and tried to force him to sign a public denunciation of his ministry.

He refused. Somehow he was able to negotiate his terms, stating only that in the past he hadn't always behaved with proper caution and had made mistakes—a rudimentary confession for a Christian. A friend asked Men how he felt about being grilled by the KGB so often, facing their questions and threats, and he said, "I'm a priest, I can talk to anybody. For me it's not difficult."[5]

When the overturn of the Soviet Union began, Men said to the young professionals, "People see perestroika as a kind of panacea. 'Ah! Here's the solution for everything!' But that's not the way it works. We are living with the consequences of a colossal historical pathology [communism]. Our Church, our Russia, have been virtually destroyed, and the damage lives on, in people's souls, in the work ethic, in the family, and in the conscience."[6]

But as the restrictions on religion lifted, Men began to broaden his ministry and move more freely. He visited schools and gave public lectures—often taking on twenty speaking engagements a month, besides Bible studies and prayer meetings and pastoral duties at his church. He put in regular appearances on radio and TV. He was instrumental in organizing an ecumenical institute in Moscow, and when he was asked how he kept up, he said, "I volunteer. God provides the time."

In the eyes of the Russian public he assumed the dimensions of Solzhenitsyn or Sakharov. And when Solzhenitsyn, then in exile in the United States, said that the single greatest hope for Russia was its underground church, he likely had Men in mind. For American journalists, Solzhenitsyn's statement simply confirmed the reactionary attitude the rumbling dinosaur revealed in his Harvard address. He was hopelessly out of touch. But Solzhenitsyn's statement proved one of the most prophetic about the change that overtook Russia.

Men told his brother that after all the years of restrictions and imposed silence he felt like "an arrow finally sprung from the bow."[7] But a darker shadow dogged him. Death threats arrived in the mail. They could have originated with the KGB or a worse tyranny—church envy. Men emphasized an ecumenicity that was not compartmentalized by denominations—a faith of universal victory in Christ—and zealots in the Orthodox Church vilified him as a secret Catholic and crypto-Jew.

Others close to Men believe an ultraconservative element of the KGB, or the church, or the two in concert, stirred members of the nationalistic group *Pamyat* to action. The Pamyat cult believes that being born a Jew is a curse and it blames all of Russia's troubles on Jews. In some of the lectures Men was giving, disruptions started appearing and one night a group shouted, "Get out, you Yid! Don't tell us about our Christian religion!"

In September of 1990 Men was asked to host a regular television show on religion and culture, scheduled for broadcast from Moscow, and also asked to accept the position of rector at the Moscow Christian Sunday University. Threatening mail arrived, and it was blunt—accept either position and you're dead. Men set the threats aside, or read them in public, meaning to undermine the authors. Parishioners and friends took it on themselves to accompany him home from public appearances, and one friend suggested he should emigrate to the West.

"Why?" Men asked. "If God hasn't turned away from me, I have to stay and serve Him. And if He *has* turned away, where could I hide?"

Western journalists took nearly three years to piece together the events of Men's last day. The following account appears, in reduced type, above Michael Meerson's chapter from 1993 on Men's life:

> In the morning twilight, the village priest opened the door and headed for the train platform less than a half-mile away. It was Sunday, and Father Aleksandr Men always caught the 6:50 A.M. *elektrichka* from his village near Zagorsk to his parish church in Novaia Derevnia, a small town outside Moscow. The priest kept walking along the asphalt path through the Semkhos Woods. Suddenly, from behind an oak, someone leapt out and swung an ax at Aleksandr Men. An ax—the traditional Russian symbol of revolt, one of the symbols of the neo-fascist group Pamyat. The blow hit Men on the back of the skull. The wound was not very deep but it severed major arteries. The killer, police sources said, grabbed the priest's briefcase and disappeared into the woods. Father Aleksandr, bleeding, stumbled toward his home, walking a full three-hundred yards to his front gate at 3-A Parkovaia Street. Along the way, two women asked if he needed help. He said no, and they left. From her window, Natasha Men saw a figure slumped near the gate pressing the buzzer. She could not quite make out who it was in the half-light. She called an ambulance. In minutes, her husband was dead.[8]

On the evening of September 8, the night before he was struck with an ax, Men gave a lecture in Moscow, with this at its at heart:

> Some ants build; some ants sow and later reap the crop; and some apes fight and have wars although they are not as cruel as people are. But nothing in nature, except for man, ever tries to think of the meaning of life. Nothing climbs above its natural physical needs. No

living creature, except for a man, is able to take a risk, and even the risk of death, for the sake of truth. Thousands of martyrs who have lived are a unique phenomenon in the history of all our solar system.

I pause at his final sentence—brimming with implications; the conventional way to express it is "martyrs who have died," and perhaps that was Men's first choice. But he had used "death" and as a biologist was speaking in a larger sense of life on earth, so "martyrs who have lived." He understood the endlessness of a martyr's death, how they live in memories and have present-day effects on others. But more than most they gain the eternality of Men's focus: Christ.

As Men had said about Jesus two months before, responding to the radio interviewer in Moscow, "*Why was he so loved and hated?*" After Men's death, the highest officials in Russia, Gorbachev and Yeltsin, denounced the brutality of his murder and demanded justice. But to this day, more than twenty years on, nobody has been accused, and not one person arrested.

All official police reports claim the motive for his murder was robbery.

How? What self-respecting thief, much less one willing to murder, would imagine a priest carrying a briefcase to a 6:00 a.m. train on Sunday a likely mark? No, what took place probably originated in the government; the hidden factions conferred and decided they had enough. They were aware of the symbolism for Russians of the icon and the ax: the one a symbol of enduring religion, the other brute force—and thus designated by Stalin to be used on Leon Trotsky.

They would smash Men the icon with the ax.

It was probably a camper's hatchet, chosen for its suitability to their plan of stealth. They had shadowed Men enough to know he walked alone on Sunday to the train to arrive in time for his morning service. A central part of the woods he passed through was deserted at that hour. One of them, no, two—cowards need company—would loiter on the asphalt path, acting as lookouts and bait—one for each arm if Men should resist. They would look confused, pretend they were lost, and hold up a scrap of paper with a map scrawled on it.

Better, a transcript of Men's talk, distributed the night before, titled, in his audacious way, "Christianity." They would approach with concern and say, "Father, is it true you really said this?"—a finger on the statement—"Martyrs who have *lived*?"

That was the cue for the one behind the oak, hidden in the spot where police found trampled underbrush, to strike—trampled in order to silence his rush and by his restless anticipation, sweating as he held himself in control and kept hidden.

But quiet, here he comes.

No one who leads a straightforward life imagines he'll be attacked from behind. Men saw the pair ahead and noticed their bedraggled state, their worn clothes and scuffed shoes and slack-lipped look of shame, a pair of the alcoholics who'd been bedding in Semkhos Park—homeless derelicts.

"Father?" one said, so sorrowful he had trouble swallowing. Since Men had been appearing in newspapers and on television, strangers recognized and spoke to him. "Father, is it true?" the other asked, and seemed unable to get his breath, his mouth slack. "Did you say this?" He held the printed pages up.

Men set his briefcase on the walk, drew his reading glasses from a pocket of his windbreaker, and slipped them on. "Now, my friends, what?"

At his voice, the hidden one sprang and struck. Men fell to the ground, silent, the hat he was wearing, gashed by the axe, lying beside him. In the silence one of the group grabbed his briefcase, snapped it open, and the assassin dropped the hatchet inside. The other snapped it closed—a sound like a pistol shot in the woods—and walked off one way while the other two took separate directions of their own, as prearranged.

In Men consciousness trembled to life. Like most who suffer a blow to the head he had no memory of the moment leading to it. He was on his way to the train for morning services and somehow fell. He got to his feet, off balance, faint, and understood he should have—he couldn't draw the thought to completion. In the distance he heard the sound of the approaching train he meant to board.

He started toward it, his legs like burrowed tree trunks shedding their substance, and realized he was pouring sweat. He put a hand to his neck and in the dim light it came away black. Perceptions reversed. Or he cut himself when he fell. In a swirl of darkness he felt suspended across the distances of time and space he imagined Jesus occupying, and then remembered his briefcase.

He swung around and when he came to the place where he'd started from, he wanted to lie down. Two women were approaching. Natasha? No. But now it was his only purpose: to see her. He shoved his hands in his pockets and steadied his walk. "Are you hurt, Father? Do you need help?"

"No, fine."

He jolted above them like a striding colossus, the riddled trunks of his legs spanning stars, his consciousness fraying like window screen giving at its edges. His heart hit his ribs so hard he knew he was dying. He squinted out one dim chink of consciousness left. *In the Garden of Gethsemane, Jesus*—the words matched his gait, drawing him along a line he couldn't otherwise manage, and he repeated them until he could see his house ahead, a light in it, its gate.

He got near the gate and knew he wouldn't make it. He forced himself to take a last step and dove, striking the palings of his fence—bars holding him from the garden where his Savior waited. He was jolted awake by that vestige of pride to the women who offered to help: *No, fine.* His body didn't respond when he tried to move but he forced a hand as far as the bell. Then the subatomic, insubstantiality of the world gave way, and he passed through the palings and everything else in the world into the solidity of everlasting light.

Natasha Men saw a man slumped against the garden gate and phoned for an ambulance, assuming she was ministering to a drunk. When the man didn't move, she felt drawn to him and cautiously opened the door. "Don't tell me," she said to a crowd already gathering, meaning she knew.

At Men's burial, in the churchyard of the parish he served for twenty-two years, a peasant-like crowd gathered with the intellectuals, and Gleb Yakunin, putting himself at risk, delivered Men's eulogy.

After the burial, a reporter for the *New York Times* found a woman praying at Men's grave. She was in her eighties, a member, he learned, of Fr. Serafim's original catacomb church. She had known Men since the day he was baptized. "The final path of this holy man was marked with his own blood!" she cried. "I remember when he was a boy and his mother showed me that he had written: 'Defeat evil by kindness.' That is exactly how he turned out."[9]

Four of Men's television shows had been taped but were somehow erased. In 1994, the Radio-1 Division of Russian State Radio began to air audio tapes of his lectures, and seventy thousand letters from listeners poured into the studios. The director of Radio-1, in a weekly report his duties demanded, wrote that because of listeners' response, the program was being moved from midnight to 10:30 p.m. and added, "The strength of the program consists in Aleksandr Men's amazing understanding of the Russian soul and his remarkable intellect of truly global range." Nothing about his Christianity.

When a parishioner of Men's heard this, he remembered that one of Men's last sermons was taken from the first chapter of the Revelation to John—when John tries to hide from the fiery, brassy incarnation of Jesus—and the parishioner said Men placed an electrifying emphasis on the statement, "I am He who lives, and was dead, and behold, I am alive forevermore."[10]

PART THREE

REALMS OF USERS

15

A STATE LAUREATE'S GRADUATION ADDRESS

Good evening, graduates, president, honored guests. I'm grateful for the opportunity to speak tonight as poet laureate. People often ask, "What *is* a poet laureate?" so let me explain, and then to business. The office of laureate varies from state to state but in North Dakota it is for life, or that's the historic precedent, although I may offer an alternative by retiring, to see a fellow poet set in place.

The institution of poet laureate stretches so far back I suspect the author of *Beowulf* was a formal or informal poet for a ruler like Hrothgar. The concept as we know it today came down from the British. An early laureate served as *versificator regis* or king's poet in the court of Richard the Lion-Hearted (1157–1199) or Coeur-de-lion as he was known in the court language of *Angleterre* in that era—that's right, French. Prior to 1369, all poetry of the English court was composed in French.

The shift to English came with Geoffrey Chaucer (1345–1400) who wrote an eulogy on the death of the wife of a member of court. Chaucer married into the aristocracy and served as *Johannes factotum* to kings such as Edward and Richard II (1367–1400). Richard was thought to be one of the first literate monarchs, anyway the first who signed his name. In 1383 Chaucer was named controller of taxes on wine and goods, and in 1394 Richard II awarded him a grant of £20; later a yearly cask of wine. It was during the reign of Richard II that Chaucer wrote *Canterbury Tales*.

Why he wasn't done in by Henry Bolingbroke, the cousin of Richard II who deposed Richard and became Henry IV, nobody knows. History names Bolingbroke the likely culprit in the death of Richard II while Richard was imprisoned at Pomfret Castle. He was assassinated or starved to death. Chaucer must have been as canny as most members of his *Canterbury Tales*. He died of natural causes in October 1400, nine months after Richard's death in January, unless the natural cause was poison.

The poet laureate became an official government position when James I appointed Ben Jonson to the office, and the British laureate, according to tradition, commemorates in poetry state celebrations and historical occasions, such as the accession of a new monarch to the throne. I suspect many early laureates provided entertainment to royalty, and perhaps injected literary substance into the doings of the court—this to say the office of poet laureate is not a modern invention.

Across the United States, state poets laureate open legislative sessions or mark the inauguration of a governor with a poem or serve as consultants or middle men between state arts councils and state legislators, but that is not so, not so far, in my home state. I was nominated for the office by the North Dakota State Library, the State Historical Society, and a coalition called The Center for The Book. Our legislature accepted the nomination and the House and Senate, in Concurrent Resolution 4039, voted to name me poet laureate. The governor conferred the office in a ceremony in March of 1995.

So a laureate is an official legal entity, or occupies an office, as it's generally known, as I have for sixteen years. According to the resolution the legislature passed—and it's a resolution, not Century Code Law—my appointment was based on the longevity and variety of my poetry and the publications it appeared in, from the *New Yorker* to journals and quarterlies to the collection *Even Tide*, published by Farrar, Straus. I have poems enough for a new book, if prose gave me time off.

I have no assigned duties but try to be available for schools and venues that can't afford to invite me to give a talk or a reading, or never thought of asking. I'm not a state employee, and until the legislative session of 2009 I did not receive a salary or stipend or reimbursement for travel. Our state legislature meets every two years for five months, enacting enough politics every other year in that brief time to satisfy everybody in the state, and over that biennium the legislature set aside a sum for ten visits to high schools. That sum was renewed in 2011.

I've written a commemorative poem for the dedication of a new Fine Arts Center at Jamestown College—a private Christian institution dating from 1883, the oldest institution of higher learning in the state, and the only school rated Tier I by *U.S. News & World Report*. I performed a poem on videotape that was played at the retirement banquet of a university president. The oddest requests rise from the assumption that writers are available to read and comment on anything anybody writes, ever, are experts in knowing how to find a place to publish, should speak on every political move of liberal enlightenment, and are expected to drop everything, including their writing, to give advice gratis—as those in medicine or lawyering or carpentry or plumbing or legislating don't.

I want to draw into greater unity the poets and writers in our state, who often work in utter obscurity. I hold workshops, I meet and encourage young writers, a few of them high-school students. When I became poet laureate, the office had been vacant for a decade, and to make sure that remains a one-time oversight, I've named a dozen associate laureates. It's also true that North Dakota is the size of Ohio and Maine put together and with the wide-open spaces between towns and villages, the associates I appoint can help spread the good news of poetry—how it can set in language our highest aspirations and at the same time strive through lows to arrive at hope, and the associates are lightning rods directing the state toward further cohesiveness, I believe, in the arts. Some are songwriters and singers like the minstrels, the earliest poets laureate of the past.

I have said, "A poet laureate should not be a mere figurehead or adornment, but called upon to add dimension to the daily grind of partisan politics." In a further statement, attempting to explain the office, I said "Most poets are rooted in the natural world, spokespersons for the inarticulate in nature as well as the wordless hopes of people putting in a long day's work—or poets should be searching for words for those sides of the world. And most poets are committed politically, in one way or another, able to present their views in a memorable matrix of words; they can, in this function of the office, serve as governing conscience for a gone-soft state."

If you wonder why no sculptor or dancer or pottery laureates exist, as a governor recently asked when he refused to sign into law legislation passed by both houses to establish an office of poet laureate in his state, I would answer that the commerce of the world, including politics, is conducted in language, not pottery or sculpture or painting, and so it will be, I suspect, to the end of time.

With this overview of poet laureate, let me suggest a significant prospect the office holds by turning to Joseph Brodsky. Brodksy is a poet who was exiled from the Soviet Union in the 1970s after serving a sentence in Siberia. He moved to America, taught and wrote poetry, was named the United States Poet Laureate, and in 1987 received the Nobel Prize for Literature. In a commencement address he gave on the subject of evil, in the year of Orwell's *1984*, he said: "One of the surest signs of danger here"—he's speaking about how to discern whether or not evil is entering your life—"is the number of those who share your views, not so much because unanimity has the knack of degenerating into uniformity as because of the probability—implicit in great numbers—that noble sentiment is being faked . . . . Evil is a sucker for solidity. It always goes for big numbers, for confident granite, for ideological purity, for drilled armies and balanced sheets."[1]

Those of you present tonight were taught in a variety of public and private schools, a few by parents, and you bring a diversity of outlooks to our gathering. You're not a homogeneous group shuttled through a series of similar classrooms like an Army brigade, as most graduating classes are, so I suspect you don't depend on the rule of peers to govern all you do. You've received a variety of teaching and this is good for you and good, too, for the diversity of our nation. An advantage of missing the regimentation of identical education so many endure is that uniformity often is, as Brodsky notes, a cloak for evil.

Merely picture uniformed soldiers marching in uniform goose-steps past a leader in a reviewing stand with his arm raised (he's in uniform, too), and you get a glimpse of the uniformity he means. Or imagine a former Soviet Union that in its unity banished Brodsky and Aleksandr Solzhenitsyn, or a perilous zone in the Middle East or Africa where people must parrot what a tyrant decrees or face death. The members of the US Department of Education, none of whom teach, set labels on education, such as No Child Left Behind or Outcome Based Education, where the outcome isn't so much a concern to teach rudimentary skills in specific subjects such as math or reading as to forge thinking into a consensus. One government goal for that kind of consensus—not of achievement—was the year 2000, and it appears they made it, so now the hope is that no child is left behind in government conformity.

Those goals are reached when the Christian community imagines, as great numbers do, that a first- or even a sixth-grade student can stand up to the one-minded dismissal of faith by adults who have day-long charge over a child for five days a week. Or that a classical education based on Plato can be resurrected, its corpse carried into the present and rebaptized, when it was abandoned at the height of the Renaissance in the work of Shakespeare, Donne, and Martin Luther.[2]

Liberal arts is not, as a young man recently stated, kind of like the painting Picasso does. A liberal education means every student receives a liberal dose of a wide spectrum of subjects from a perspective that is either objective or includes several sides. But it appears to mean, now, that you're educated to be a liberal, global citizen in agreement with every other global citizen on one-and-the-same wavelength as defined in Washington DC, or at the United Nations. You're educated in evil.

The essential moral law of Christian teaching, to love your neighbor as yourself, has devolved in America to another level: whatever I can get by with is OK as long as my friends or office mates agree. This is the law enthroned in civic and public affairs, in extracurricular sex, and the law daily practiced by corrupt elected officials and corporate heads—also talking heads on corporate television news. A true consensus of evil arrives when government and society or both excuse a president for sexual abuse of power because the economy is good; or refuse to criticize another for fear of being labeled a racist.

Joseph Brodsky died several years ago, and in the commencement address I mention, in the telltale year when Big Brother took over but people were too busy watching television to notice, Brodsky said, "The surest defense against Evil is extreme individualism, originality of thinking, whimsicality, even—if you will—eccentricity."[3]

He then turns his listeners, the graduates of Williams College, to the Sermon on the Mount, where Jesus instructs his followers to turn the other cheek. But if we stop there, Brodsky warns, we may merely end up with a bruised face, and may have missed the heart of Jesus's teaching. Tolstoy and his disciples, Gandhi and Martin Luther King, went astray here, Brodsky says, by halting at the idea of passive resistance. No, he says, and recounts his experience in a prison labor camp where he was sent, as poet and Jew, because the originality of his person and his practice of poetry caused the Soviet state to condemn him as a "parasite." No, he says, don't stop there—and it's a joy to watch this Russian-Jewish poet stride into Jesus's teaching with the brio of a born exegete—you must also let your enemy take your coat and cloak, and if he asks you to go a mile you must go two, and then Brodsky says, leaping to the New Testament application we need to hear: You must overcome evil with good.[4]

Aleksandr Men also understood that emphasis.

Education is not the antidote to social ills, the No-Doz to evil and daily responsibility. Doing good to others, loving your neighbor as yourself, and not only that, loving you enemies, praying for those who despise you and treat you with disdain and scorn, even to the point of wishing you were dead, that is the answer and that is the antidote.

It's a hard lesson to learn, especially for adults, but it's the decisive element in education. If you haven't been brought further along that path, you haven't entered the mystery that causes the universe to cohere: love for the loveless.

No religion but Christianity has the audacity to ask that much of you because of its namesake, Christ. No religion dares to say God became man; that this God-man participated in the creation of the cosmos and was the Lamb slain before it was created, although that happened in real time, too. It was his sacrifice of love for others, even his enemies, that gathers listeners at mountains for eternity.

The fullness of that provision before worlds were created is, to a poet and creator of fiction, hair-raising—like having a best-seller before you write page one. The literal meaning of the Greek for resurrection is to stand up, and its truth should make your hair stand up. Although you were evil, *as I was*, God's good was handed to us. Jesus never insisted on his right to be called God or told everybody about the wonderful work he'd done, so he could lord it over others. He became a servant, humbling himself further, and when he was reviled he didn't strike back; in the midst of torture he didn't threaten his torturers with *I'll get you some day*, but was obedient to sacrifice his good for our evil.

Set your education on him.

Joseph Brodsky was exiled to Siberia, to a slave labor camp where the inmates had to chop a certain quota of wood each day. Rather than setting aside his ax at the quota he kept chopping and refused to stop, returning good for evil through a day and night until the director of the camp grew so uneasy he asked him to quit. Evil was overmastered. Anybody who acts as Brodsky did is living out the example set by the true leader of the world.

The essential task is the moment you're called on to return good for evil, and it's often a moment of small, even minute detail rather than one of world-changing grandeur that many imagine. If you master that task you'll be a leader in your time and face further hurdles. So may the comfort-inducing Spirit that carries you through time carry you with a noise as joyful as the bells once fastened to every horse's harness, ringing out "Holiness to the Lord!" And may the pans and bowls of your households resound with a resonating clatter as you live out your lives in peace with others, as much as it's in you, and may each of you say to the all-hating world, I will overcome every iota of hate I encounter with good.

You hear that out there?

16

A CONCERN FOR THE
STATE OF INDIAN AFFAIRS

In 1959, the American critic and panjandrum of literary and cultural affairs, Edmund Wilson, published *Apologies to the Iroquois*. With the appearance of Wilson's book nobody can deny it was then that word went out to whites, for any who were willing to listen, about unrest within the Six Nations—the Mohawks, Senecas, Onondagas, Oneidas, Cayugas, and Tuscaroras—over the white will.

The territories of the Six Nations extend from Canada into the northeastern lower forty-eight, and it wasn't only those nations but others as diverse as the Miccosukees and Hopis, along with tribes in North, South, and Central America that were beginning to band together, Wilson says, in an unrest that was bringing about radical reassessment in Native Nations and civil governments—after a century of essential passivity. The basis of the unrest was, to put it bluntly, dirty dealing: treaties broken, land grants dishonored, native land and native burial grounds flooded by yet another water diversion project, as if it weren't human beings or their remains being diverted. No political party or administration is entirely free of blame.

From Edmund Wilson's time, if not Fenimore Cooper's, a tradition of advocacy for Native Nations has existed among writers, especially novelists, including Rudy Wiebe, Thomas Berger, Evan Connell, and Peter Matthiessen, to name some North Americans. Matthiessen hit home with perhaps the greatest impact in the nineties, with the publication of *Killing Mister Watson* and the reissue of *In the Spirit of Crazy Horse*, originally published a decade earlier. All the original copies of that book (except a few sent to critics and friends) were shredded in 1983 before distribution could begin by a court injunction filed by the attorney general, soon-to-be governor, then United States representative from South Dakota, William Janklow. In 2003 Janklow was convicted of manslaughter when his car, traveling at a speed judged to exceed ninety miles an hour, ran a stop sign and decimated a motorcyclist.

The trek of the writerly or literary tradition is apparent in the summary of a treaty quoted in Rudy Wiebe's *The Temptations of Big Bear*, recipient of the Governor General's Award in Canada for 1973:

> Her Majesty agreed to set aside reserves of land for them [one need not guess who] in a ratio of one square mile for each five-member family; to maintain schools if they desired; not to deprive them of their habitual hunting rights; to distribute monies of five dollars per person every year, with fifteen dollars for each counselor and twenty-five dollars for each chief, to provide ammunition and twine for nets . . . [and so on into a list of particular supplies that runs half a page]. On their part, the Indians agreed to choose their reserves and behave themselves according to Her law, as good and loyal subjects of Her Majesty the Queen.[1]

In *Fools Crow*, a novel by a Montana Blackfeet, James Welch, the American cavalry officer, General Sully, arrives at Four Horns Agency on the Milk River to confront a few of the Pikuni, or Blackfeet, about a particularly heartless raid (by a heartless brave's band, as Welch makes clear) on a group of whites:

> "Now"—Sully leaned back and faced the chiefs directly—"it has been the history of the Blackfeet to commit these crimes and then sneak off across the medicine line into Canada, knowing full well that we could not pursue them into that country. There they have felt secure enough to sell horses and buy whiskey and rifles and generally live high on the hog until they felt it was safe to return . . ."

Rides-at-the-door stared out one of the windows while the sergeant's voice droned dutifully on in translation. He could see only the tops of the roofs and the flag, which now hung limply from the pole. He looked at the sky beyond the flag, but he couldn't tell if it was blue or gray or white.[2]

We should note the concurrence of the last half of Welch's final sentence with the first sentence of a story, "The Open Boat," by Stephen Crane, in which an isolated group under duress is forced to consider its chance of survival: "None of them knew the color of the sky."[3] No government representative or Army general knew at the time the condition of the people he was speaking to, in this clear echo of Crane. Against the sky, limp, is the emblem of national identity of the *other*, the Napikwan or Washichu flag.

Wiebe often mentions a flag at treaty gatherings or meetings, as when Governor Morris confronts the Cree chiefs at the opening of *The Temptations of Big Bear*. Here it's a Canadian, John McDougall, who claims that those on the other side of a national boundary, or medicine line, the Americans, sell arms and ammunition and whiskey to the Indians.[4] Rather than enter into a dispute over the two nations that have lived in peace with each other longer than most, or attempt to adjudicate which side was worse, we can assume that supplies like this were sold to Native Nations and tribes of the Americas by members of a European culture.

Welch's novel opens before any penetration of those cultures (or *contact*) takes place in Blackfeet territory. Later, when Boss Ribs, the medicine man of the band Welch is commemorating, speaks to Fools Crow about becoming his successor, Welch notes, in a particularly arresting moment in the novel: "Some children ran by, leaving a trail of laughter in the shadowy lodge. Each man remembered that he had been a child once, had laughed the same way, at nothing but his own joy."[5]

Welch, who was raised on reservations in Montana, is aware of the Trail of Tears, the designation given by natives to the removal of the Cherokee Nation from southeastern United States to Indian Territory. Indian Territory is now Oklahoma, although it was set aside to remain a native settlement in perpetuity. *Trail of tears* could as well be applied to Chief Joseph's trek from Oregon to Canada, then farther east and south with his dwindling band until the army settled it at Fort Leavenworth, Kansas.

Welch contrasts that tearful dislocation with an era of the Blackfeet, circa 1850, when children were heard from the interior of a shadowy buffalo-skin lodge to leave a *trail of laughter*. Fools Crow and Boss Ribs, hearing the laughter, remember how it was when, as children, each in his freedom "had laughed the same way, at nothing but his own joy."

Laughter is a leitmotif that occurs through the novel. When Fools Crow starts to fall asleep before he visits the otherworld of a vision, "he felt himself drifting to a place closer to the sleeping song. And then he heard the chatter and laughter of children and let himself go."[6] And when he meets the person responsible for the sleeping song, a woman in white buckskin who serves as guide during his dream vision, "he listened to the woman's song and he heard, beyond her voice, the noise like a distant waterfall of children laughing."[7]

Here the accumulated voices have attained the concussive force of a waterfall, but a distant one. Already the joy is being consigned to the past, to a phenomenon of the natural world.

More than one Indian I've known has said directly or expressed by his or her attitude, Where has the laughter of the early time gone? I don't figure this as a descent into nostalgia but akin to tragedy, and the response of a sufferer of tragedy is often anger, as with Owl Child in *Fools Crow* and Big Bear, the title character of Wiebe's novel. The stoic reserve of a native, as reported by European contact and enshrined in Hollywood, is really a report on silent anger building. Incursions from Europe had spread in every direction—the East Coast, Florida, California, Mexico—by the 1500s, and most incursions caused a dislocation, meaning a continental move, in many Native Nations. A central source of the anger is the way the vitality of freedom on native natural landscapes was robbed from Native Nations.

Land was taken, along with freedom to travel where a tribe might wish; lives were taken, and in instances an entire way of life, as with the lodge-building agricultural Mandans—their lodges standing up to North Dakota weather for generations, more durable than the Algonquin's. That life is gone, along with every trace of their villages that once lined the upper Missouri, except for some government reconstructions.

Forgiveness, resolution, restitution—all part of native tradition—all these, too, were taken or at least encroached on in the case of Crow Dog before the United States Supreme Court in 1883. As great a loss might be every Indian's inability to escape the bombarding influence of the presiding culture of bureaucratic hegemony and falsely defined political correctness—the superior attitude of a culture that will, for example, decide that Indians should be called Native Americans, rather than the historic names of the nations they used, and then employ the designation in their agendas and academic courses, or use native names for sports teams, the worst The Washington Redskins. And there's the other side—banishing the native name of a sports team without consulting the nation named to find whether it feels pride or satisfaction or shame or denigration at the use of the name.

American Indian Movement, Red Power, First Nations, Native Americans—these are the names that come down from those in precincts of power, in a generalized abandonment of distinctions. I suggest, in the manner of Vine DeLoria—Indian lawyer and spiritual leader—that whites need not go on their hands and knees in guilt over their ancestor's acts; they offend enough in the present. When I look at the panoply of contemporary Indian fiction, from M. Scott Momaday to James Welch to Leslie Marmon Silko to Linda Hogan and Louise Erdrich and Diane Glancy and Sherman Alexie, I sense an icy minimalist seethe of emotion (evolving to fuller expression in some) that can switch in a second to anger, as in Erdich's recent *Roundhouse*.

Anyone who reads the literature can't help coming away with the sense that the deracination of an entire interior life, not merely a race, has taken place—an interior life of the kind depicted in the recurring laugher seen in Welch, or Nanapush's need to talk his way out of death in Erdrich's *Tracks*. A heritage was refined away by a process that many, even in the twenty-first century, view as necessary and healthy, and the process is, in a single word, *education*.

Or education, as defined by professionals, that is not collegial give and take, but an ideology that insists something must be inserted in your head. Indian boarding schools are the most obvious instruments of that indoctrination.

The British novelist and poet, John Wain, says in his biography of Samuel Johnson that

> Johnson, as an individual, was highly independent and unbiddable. He did not fit smoothly into any system. Intellectually, on the other hand, he approved of systems. Free of any starry-eyed notion of the natural goodness of man, he insisted on the need to keep up the outward forms and conventions that act as some check on man's natural lawlessness. And he knew all about lawlessness because he felt its power in his own anarchic impulses.
>
> In this we see something of Johnson's generous self-forget-fulness, his power to reach intellectual conclusions on impersonal grounds. Most people are entirely lacking in this quality. The average "intellectual," especially, is the reverse of intellectual in his handling of theoretical questions. His deductive chain starts from self and ends at self. Because he has been ill at ease within the family, he wants to abolish the family. Because the power structure of his society does not automatically waft him to a position of unrestricted authority, he wants to abolish the power structure. The unspoken premise at the back of all his reasoning is that the world to be striven for is a world in which *he* will get what he wants.[8]

Education at these intellectual fonts isn't an advantage to writers, either, especially writers like Welch and Erdrich. The *canonmeisters* tend to enthrone an established culture, a literary one, over the inborn intuitiveness that is a writer's natural gift. What I'm saying is partly metaphor, but only partly. The distance the reader can encounter in the work, for instance, of Erdrich, of Chippewa and German descent, isn't the detachment of a scholar but a tricked hunter in a fury of silence following the blood trail home. Erdrich has degrees from Dartmouth and Johns Hopkins, has taught at Dartmouth, and with each book seems to express with increasing clarity the deracination one half of her heritage has undergone.

The detachment of a scholar is truly rare, since any scholarly composition (especially a thesis or dissertation for an advanced degree) must first be approved by an academic superior and then prove a point or argue into clarity a thesis, often a pet theory of a committee chair. So an intellectual's detachment approximates the detachment of a prosecutor pressing for a guilty verdict.

That kind of argumentation is the opposite of the tone expressed in the work of Welch and Erdrich and, as far as it goes, Michael Dorris. Dorris, too, is a novelist, *was* a novelist, married to Erdrich, co-collaborator with her on *The Crown of Columbus*—here I have to stop to wonder whether any honest intellect can sidestep the question of whether Dorris's death at his own hand doesn't suggest a rage at deracination that became unbearable to live with in the academic world of smiling, calculating, white-folk networks, poised as if in patience to see him fail.

All three writers are servants to their characters and few characters serve the writer's needs. Erdrich's detached perspective, which can arrive as iciness, seems the necessary evaluating distance of the poet or autobiographical novelist, both of whom work with similar material in the same context: unpinning the impingement of the experience of the world on an internal state and setting it in the words of metaphor. This attitude requires the poised and evaluating scrutiny of a hunting cat, a quality apparent also in Colette, farm girl gone Parisian, and is a form of self-protection.

The daily experience of a writer of this kind—John Updike is an example—can become a kind of blight: perceptions and thoughts and emotions and pleasant or unpleasant communal experiences are continually strained through a grid of consciousness that attempts to find for them their proper words. Particular language is the medium writers use to rehearse their inner take on the world for a reader. They *enact* language on a page, rather than letting it fly free in an everyday situation and their use of words sets free personal takes and convictions, just as inclinations in faith, or lack of them, draw others to the views they express. The omnivorous state of this sensibility, once it grows, is probably a reason too many writers drink too much—to shut off even for an hour the endlessly chattering and screening activity of that inner machine.

This, I suspect, has affinities to the inner world of a native responding to the natural world as outsiders cannot. We receive only glimpses or flashes of this from writers of a higher order, such as Welch and Erdrich, and only because they relate that inner life in a roundabout way, through the medium of a European language. It would be helpful to Native Nations if more members were willing to confront the prejudice and pitfalls of the academy and become not only students but lecturers and professors, as I suggest below.

The exchange between the two could lead to further understanding of the views of the other, especially if the outlooks were presented in the metaphor of stories and tales and legends, so that each side learned from exposure to the other's unchained narrative. Politics and polemics and prejudices and academic tinkering would have to be abandoned in the mutual endeavor. Wisdom and knowledge and understanding, especially of the workings of the natural world, as in the pyrotechnics of Vine DeLoria and M. Scott Momaday, could flow in the direction of understanding in the exchange. The cultural dialogue should include the question of whether a tribal elder or holy person can teach courses for credit without the usual academic degrees—minor reparation after the abuses of boarding schools.

I submitted a proposal along those lines to the academic dean and the English Department at the University of North Dakota in 2004, before the school became legally embroiled, years later, over its "Fighting Sioux" nickname:

> I believe reparation must continue to be made in substance to our Native Nations for treaties dishonored or broken, land given and taken away, at federal, state, and local—let's say, rancher—levels, and at the university. The University of North Dakota in particular, as the intellectual flagship of the state, should be taking the lead in this arena.

You might see it as reparation for that other arena, the skating rink [Ralph Englestad hockey stadium, then recently completed, and a focus for both sides on the Fighting Sioux name].

We should not try to quell a few of the areas of hostility between white and native races, but should be abolishing and destroying every trace of hostility—this is a human rights issue—in ourselves, first, so we're fit to help others along the route. To start down that route, UND needs to make a sweeping gesture, and not just a gesture, but a notable public stand.

The potential is Lincolnesque; the university can help emancipate Native brothers and sisters from intellectual captivity. It can affirm to them that the bureaucratic structure of the university will welcome Native wisdom into its tiers, whether the possessor of wisdom has an advanced degree or not—even, indeed, any degree. The English Department now has that opportunity at its doorstep; it's been given the go-ahead to hire a poet of accomplishment, and we've met Mark Turcotte [who participated in the UND Writer's Conference that year], not only a Native American but a native son of the state. His poetry, wisdom, humor, perspicuity, and ability to teach are extraordinary.

Reparation is meant to give satisfaction for wrong or injury done, and usually seems to arrive with a kind of buttered-on condescension. To consider Turcotte for a position would not, I feel, be a newer form of that kind of condescension, because it demands a giving way or a giving away of cherished academic ideals. But the source of those ideals is a white European tradition that asserted itself as superior over an indigenous culture—mostly with rifles.

As I mentioned in a kind of footnote to another proposal your chair sent to the dean, I feel that the hire of a Native of the caliber of Mark Turcotte has the potential to add such enhancement to the department it would set it above any in the state and surrounding area, all the way past Minneapolis. We have here one of the largest Native populations of any state in the continental United States, when you include all of Standing Rock, with a central administration in North Dakota, at Fort Yates, and no English Department or writing program or arts organization in the area has ever offered a beckoning hand in quite the way this would to our Native residents.

The English Department has the opportunity to take a groundbreaking step of a new kind in its hire of this extraordinary poet.

This proposal was turned aside with little discussion except "no credentials," and no consideration of Turcotte's publications.

In *The Crown of Columbus*, one of the most interesting novels of recent years, qualities of warmth and humor and a generous maturity are present, unremarked upon by most reviewers, to a degree not found in quite the same way in Erdrich's earlier work—though a sense of it rises through *Tracks*, the novel in which she most explicitly explores her native heritage—and all those qualities are present in *A Yellow Raft in Blue Water*, Michael Dorris's first novel.

The Crown of Columbus suggests a solution to the unrest and duress of the Native Nations of the Americas as no other novel I know. It is concerned with a search for Columbus—a scholarly search for a portion of the manuscript of his journals, which will lead either the right or the wrong party to the object that crowned the end of Columbus's life, the crown of the book's title. It is also a search for Columbus himself, the person who, perhaps more than any other, affected the settlement and makeup of, anyway, the South American continent.

The central character of the novel, Vivian Twostar, a member of the faculty at Dartmouth, comes across a clue to Columbus in a portion of the manuscript journal of his first voyage to the "Indies." Vivian is ultimately helped in her research by a previously disaffected Indian student, who years ago hid an object in one of the libraries at Dartmouth—a college that encouraged the enrollment of American Indians for a century. Vivian Twostar would like Columbus to catch it in the neck, as readers may suspect, but *The Crown of Columbus* takes a transcontinental distance from simplistic solutions.

Vivian, once married to a native, has a teenage son, and during the course of the novel she falls under the thrall of Roger Williams, a member of the Dartmouth faculty, a poet, and, of course, a WASP. Roger is writing an extended poem about Columbus's early life (actually composed by Erdrich), planning to coincide its completion with the quincentennial of Columbus' American contact in 1492. During this year, as Vivian pursues heinous Columbus as "discoverer," she begins to carry Roger's child, and eventually moves into his house, though at first she dislikes, even detests him. She has the child, a daughter, Violet, and the ménage of four, including Vivian's teenage son, Nash, form a family.

We begin to see how resolution and reconciliation, rather than a patrimony issued from above by the BIA or government bureaucracy, can be achieved, anyway in a literary work. Unselfish personal reconciliation is the only way to undo the knot for centuries called "the Indian problem." Before the novel is over, Vivian has to deal with a man as unscrupulous about family and property and promises as any federal administration has been to Native Nations, and nearly loses her life.

And Roger nearly loses his, sunk in an unscalable bat cave for the same term Jonah spent in a whale, or the days of Christ in his tomb. I won't reveal the interleaving complexity of the book's plot, or the series of stunning turns through its last chapters, but I want to give some sense of its tone of resolution. Near its end, Roger writes, "I sometimes remember that vast depth [the bat cave] where I found my own darkness.

> As I feel for the stair rails, the way to my office, as I tap my hands along the walls, I think of that world below. I was lost, but now am living in the daily heaven of an unexpected life. I was a stranger to my family, to my daughter, but now am found. I sing the body electric instead of the stranded mind. For I've changed.
>
> One can change. I've learned that. One can accommodate the habits of others.[9]

One can change; that is the pivot and message of *The Crown of Columbus*. Each one can change on an individual level and accommodate personal habits in the lives of others. When the biographer Wain points out that the intellectual strives in a world in which he selfishly hopes to gain what *he* wants, the subject of his biography offers an antidote: "Johnson's premise, on the contrary, is that the world must arrange itself in a way that unites the majority of its inhabitants and gives them a chance to live decent, peaceable and useful lives; and that he, and people like him, will then take their chance of happiness within that order."[10]

Within that order, what must be done is where there have been depredations, where treaties have been broken and promises buried in documents hidden in archives, whether by state or municipal or national governments, restitution must be made. The American government has to unlimber itself and do this, as they have for imprisoned Japanese Americans, none of whom had to live for generations in the concentration camps commonly called Indian reservations.

The extent of that restitution on a personal level, however, is every American's responsibility, not governments' alone. And once restitution is made, the responsibility on the other side is to forgive, as Vivian Twostar forgives Roger Williams and, in a larger sense, ultimately forgives even Columbus for claiming a native habitation as a colony of far-off Europe. Then each must say to the other, with the integrity only individuals can foster, *Now where do we go?* The governing premise must be that *we can change*, all of us; and each must change if we are to enter the state of mutual regard necessary to regain a united nation.

17

A VIEW OF THE ETHICS RELATED TO WRITING

Nearly all ethical systems and formulas fall into one of two categories, either ethics of intention or ethics of outcome. Ethicists are divided whether the motive of an act or the result of an act makes the act moral. Agape combines both. Agape is a motive of good will for the other that is rooted in God's love. It never intends evil, but rather hates evil and wills good for the other. A problem with intention-based ethics, however, is that they cannot guarantee outcomes. Sometimes what we intend for good works for other than good. When we act according to agape, however, we can be assured that our action conforms to God's nature, and will be used for the fulfillment of his eternal will. Agape is a commitment to a course of action that is divinely inspired, for whatever results from agape is the will of God.[1]

James R. Edwards

How wonderful to address a group of young writers in the upper room of the Algonquin, where I was once you—a young writer sitting in New York City at the age of twenty-two. In the space of recent years the ethics of writing and reportage have so often been in the spotlight you might think I'm taking my direction from headlines or the nightly news. No, the business of writing has always presented ethical dilemmas. We can begin with the scandal a few years ago at the local banner newspaper, the *New York Times*, the Gray Lady as she was once known for her decorous, mannerly, and classically reserved tone, with every news story adhering to the traditions and ethics of journalism, from objective reportage to jog-trot pyramiding.

The Gray Lady lived into the eighties, when opinion began to creep into news articles, and then the actions of a young reporter removed two reigning editors from her staff—editors are the overseeing writers and rewriters and publishers are the businessmen, generally. So the cream of the *Times* writing staff, according to *Times'* judgment, gauged by advancement, are gone, including the higher senior editor who oversaw the editor overseeing the young writer.

A few years later it was obvious that illegal documents were manufactured by Dan Rather (or perhaps a member of his staff) and the participants should have gone to jail for forgery. But anchors now are celebrities and can get by with hijinks as egregious as we've seen in members of congress, presidents, and football and basketball stars. Next came revelations of invented stories at CNN, a plagiarized article from the *Wall Street Journal*, down to the untruthful yammering and yelling of opinionated opinion makers, who have no interest in hard news, only polemics, lately mostly women at stage center every night, on most major networks, while portions of the public still believe they're hearing news.

A surprising element as an outsider were the statements at the *New York Times* of the editor who oversaw the invented stories of the young reporter and confessed he had kept the reporter on, even encouraged him, in spite of errors of commission and omission he recognized in his writing—factual errors, no facts, invented facts, and all the rest until the young reporter fell into outright plagiarism and invention. The editor kept him on, he said, because of guilt about a tradition of prejudice in the region of the United States where he grew up. Prejudice for him continued to exist, in his mind anyway, and he apparently believed he was compensating for it at the expense, meanwhile, of professional standards. Those standards are gauged by ethics.

I am, you are, we all are flawed. We carry prejudices or resistances of one kind or another and eventually have to admit our fallibility—one of the domains of maturity—and take ourselves in hand, so our flaws don't cloud our ability to carry on an ethical life of daily decisions, and in this way prevent any remaining personal stain from infecting the lives of others.

"Don't lie," I sometimes admonish young writers. More pertinent to the dimensional application a writer has to consider are the words in the language of the next-to-last of the government-banned commandments: Don't bear false witness against your neighbor. What an artful summation and clear instruction, with not a mention of "lie" or the lying that a false witness employs or incites!

Its words speak especially to the writer and say, on the simplest level, Don't write anything about anybody you wouldn't say to anybody face-to-face. Don't say anything about anybody to another person that you wouldn't say to the person you're writing about. And above all, don't falsify reports about a person, or descend into slander or the legal realm of libel—slanderous words that appear in print. Those are the ethics that rest under every form of writing, including fiction, and *Don't lie* is probably the easiest way to gain entry into the slowing of thought a writer should enter, a meditative state, before he or she begins to set words down in sentences.

Novelists often alter characters or circumstances drawn from an original, in stories other than journalism can be, to protect people who might have exposed themselves in moments of personal distress or joy, the writer guided by the knowledge, *You must live with the consequences of your conscience.*

If you continue to view writing as your chosen career, you, too, will face ethical quandaries, maybe not of the magnitude of the young reporter at the *Times* or Dan Rather, and these will bring about a series of moral decisions, as the young journalist and his editors were compelled to undergo. Dan Rather was removed from his position by CBS brass but continues to adopt a naysaying, sheepish innocence.

Ethics may be viewed as the ability to make mistakes alongside the desire to right them. You hear people say, "There are the ethics for your personal life, and the ethics of your job or profession—besides the laws of the universe, the general physical laws and the laws of tradition and prohibition and society—and seldom do the twain meet."

Ethics derive from a standard, without internal and external distinctions, or ethics can change as often as clouds on a windy day. Here is a dilemma or quandary young people undergo; there is no standard, all is a blur, yet I must be "open" to every opinion, however destructive or arcane. Some who meddle in ethics tend to relate this practice of random inclusion to the theory of relativity, which Einstein meant to refer to particles in motion as related to the speed of light, not morals.

In "Introduction: Our Virtue," the first sentence of Alan Bloom's *The Closing of the American Mind*, he states, "There is one thing a professor can be absolutely certain of: almost every student entering the university believes, or says he believes, that truth is relative."[2] This concept has echoed down the corridors of thought for centuries, from the time of Pilate's question to Jesus, "*What is truth?*"

The irony of his question, which appears in a narrative that uses the word "truth" twice as much as the other three accounts added together, the Gospel of John, is that Pilate addresses it to the only epitome of truth to inhabit the planet. Either you believe that or you don't, and, in extenuation, you may be a Pilate or you may not. In the questing disbelief many today champion as heroic, the quest can center on formless mishmash, as in deciding whether the "truth" of the bag lady on the corner isn't as valid as Plato or Pascal or, indeed, the Bible. Government entities often reverse their truth, *the* truth as they view it, daily.

I attended the first national conference of state poet laureates in New Hampshire in 2003, and members of the press were waiting for the arrival of Amiri Baraka, the laureate from New Jersey who was in the throes of being removed from office by his state legislature. He had written a poem about the Twin Towers' destruction in which he suggested, in a number of lines, that Israeli nationals had advance warning of the disaster.

He never appeared at the conference—perhaps a warning reached him—and members of the press were disappointed, disenchanted, at the minimum. Two of them gave impassioned speeches on America and its president's mismanaging of foreign affairs, primarily focusing on the war in Iraq—these were reporters, mind you, speaking during a panel discussion of poets, the event they were covering. At a break in their polemics, I asked one who kept referring to Baraka, "Do you believe what he wrote is true?"

"It's true for *him*," he said.

Which left me wondering; if I invented a scene from the war in Iraq, say, which was true for me, would that be truth? Could I sell it? A month later that is roughly what the *Times* reporter did—wrote a story cast as an interview about a hostage rescued during that war, a young woman he never took the time to meet or speak to, much less interview.

Ethical decisions aren't often clear cut. I once met a writer who was working on the biography of a well-known diplomat to China, much older than he, of a nineteenth-century cast. The writer asked if I would look at an early chapter. I was surprised to find it written entirely in the first person: "I woke to a radiant red sky and set to rights my files of dispatches from Chiang Kai Check before I sat to breakfast that April morning of 1951." I'm making this up, as I have the subject of the biography, to illustrate how the book went: I did this, I did that, at such and such a time.

I asked the writer if the biographee supplied him with recordings or diaries of his activities, or if he interviewed him that extensively, and he said, No, he had talked with him, and the fellow had written things down, even tried an autobiography on his own that didn't work, so he turned the project over to the writer, who also had done some of his own research, he said.

"But this is in the first person. The reader will assume it's written by the person you're writing about."

"But it isn't," he said. "I wrote it."

"Is it ethical, then, to set it in first person?"

"Hmm," he said, "I hadn't thought of that."

A decade later I wrote a biography in the third person but incorporated long quotes from the subject of the biography. These were in first person, of course, and in the introduction to the book I wrote, "After experimenting with several ways of telling the story, I found it best suited my ear when, as much as possible it unfolded in Harold's [the biographee's] voice, colored by his choice of words. Because of the dozens of interviews [he gave] over the years, I had at hand two or three versions of each story—always the same but with fuller detail on occasion. So every speech of his that appears within quotation marks is actually a reconstruction, a palimpsest arranged and edited from several."

I interviewed Harold myself for a year, and had transcripts of our tape-recorded talks typed up, but now and again he said things as we were walking along, off the cuff, and sometimes I took notes on these and sometimes didn't. Here and there I included moments I held only in memory, which I tend to mistrust, and once wrote, "Memory is a magpie after chips of colored glass and ribbon rather than the upright accuracy of objective sequence."

I felt I was skating on the melting edge of ethics by including remarks whose only reference occasionally was my memory. I eased my conscience by asking Harold to read the manuscript—he read, in fact, three drafts of it—and to mark any passages where he felt the tone was off, or sensed I was putting words in his mouth, or that he hadn't used in a particular instance. You should get an idea of how involved this can become.

Harold didn't make a mark. He asked me, however, to cut two particular scenes that dealt not with him but an acquaintance, Gene Autry, who happened to be my favorite cowboy when I was growing up. Autry was once a hard drinker, as I learned from Harold's stories, and I mentioned instances that only Harold had seen, and he didn't feel it was fair to Autry to set them in the light that I had, those days now past.

Did I tell him the accuracy and art of my book, in its march toward verity, demanded I leave in those details—the ethical aesthetics of the writer? The biography after all wasn't about Autry, but the entrepreneur Harold whose first-person voice I used, and I had accumulated enough years of my own to discern how the prejudice of youth against authority, against a heroic paternal figure, or the staid or elderly, had caused the boy who once revered Gene Autry to ax away the camouflage and leave him, flaws revealed, a public drunk.

Charity is the other side of the coin of ethical concern, as the subject of the biography taught me, and I cut the scenes of Gene Autry as he requested.

In a philosophical sense I believe the Greeks were right or anyway tending in a helpful direction with their idea that ethics and aesthetics (the critical or laudatory definitions of art) are inseparable. As a writer and editor and professor I'm called on to say whether a piece of writing is good or bad, equally so when it's my own. The qualities that identify it as bad are self-satisfaction, inaccuracy that leads to distortion, lack of precision, lack of passion, lack of depth, lack of even-handedness, superficial focus, greater concern for the roll on one's tongue of the prose rather than the people portrayed, and on and on—all of which suggest a lack of charity—a series of internal ethical flaws or, to get downright biblical about most of the instances, sin.

Spelling and grammar I can fix, but what do I do about the person behind the words, whether a news story or a fiction, when I have to wonder whether a character fault hasn't spoiled the entire enterprise, especially if the person is me? I must say at the minimum, *This doesn't work.*

When writers insist that they deal in mere facts, as writers will about a genre, especially reportage and history, we should understand that a bare fact is exactly that—bare of meaning, a mere shingle of information for the roof of a house or barn not built. This is true as long as a fact sits outside a context. Once you start uniting a series of facts to arrange them in a story, intellectual or temporal or both, the story line that forms will reveal your interpretation of the facts you started with, the ones you gathered or omitted, and will alert an attentive reader to the accuracy or inexcusable tilt or even spin to your interpretation of those mere "facts."

The best writers render the proper weight and authority, within a context, to each fact, not ignoring facts that might clash with a theory they happen to hold, which is something else altogether—a supposition formed before a person examines any facts or begins writing—which calls to mind the biographer who told me he wrote the story he wanted to tell and later filled in the facts.

Writers are aware that facts, which are formed of words, can be sifted, sorted, set aside, deleted, altered, inflated, or shaved down to achieve a slant that matches the writer's preconceptions or ambitions or, worse, a scurrilous theory. A universal fact surrounding every living entity is the cosmos, available to the eye of the most and least educated across the planet, sustaining every person in its equipoise within a network of infinite precision. Who sees it my way?—that hidden attributes of the creator are revealed in its daily activity? that this mystery informs or confounds my writing from the first, before I came across the passage in St. Paul's epistle to the Romans?

The universal fact behind Paul's shocking declaration is that a greater meaning to existence, the hint to a truth sustaining the cosmos, is available to anybody observing the natural world, even the sky over a city. So that none, Paul writes, has an excuse for saying there's no more to life than one can see or touch or taste or feel, or in any personal individual manner *sense*.

This is the mystery (if I may, since it has been called that by a reviewer or two) at the center of my writing, or anyway the best of it. *So I believe*, I should add. I can't remember an editor, whether at the *New Yorker* or *Atlantic* or *Paris Review* or any publication I worked with say to me, "Now, Larry, we have to cut this because it deals with religion or your personal faith."

That never happened.

What did happen is a young editor at the *New Yorker* asked me, after the magazine accepted a story, if I felt it was necessary to suffer in order to receive a revelation of faith of the kind a character of mine exhibits at the end of story. I said, No, I didn't think it was necessary, no, but one's faith might *bring* suffering; that was a possibility. I was thinking of Jesus saying, "If anyone would come after me, let him deny himself and take up his cross daily and follow me" and an apostle's injunction that "it has been granted to you that for the sake of Christ you should not only believe in him but also suffer for his sake."[3] But the question opened the opportunity to discuss with the editor, who was Jewish, some of the meanings and uses of faith, which he saw as a "safety net"—to use his expression. The point is we sat and talked in a civilized fashion about faith in his office high above New York City.

I have never understood the fascination of the modern church and a large portion of the Christian population with fantasy. Fantasy and science fiction are commonly used as a means of confronting a troubling or complex social issue in a roundabout way instead of dealing with it directly. Tolstoy and to a lesser degree Dostoyevsky and Turgenev, to set this outside American fiction, deal with these issues head on. I believe that fears of nuclear annihilation caused the outpour of science fiction in the 1950s, the glory years of that genre, as if to say, Can't science deal with its deathly inventions?—just as the innate fear of ultimate personal annihilation forced to the surface the "undead" stories of Edgar Allen Poe.

That trend is carried forward in the present by the popular vampire and zombie and werewolf novels and films that say to a disaffected, burned-out, deracinated, and homogenized generation of little or no hope, stranded in a culture of monotone meaninglessness, any possibility of a hereafter discarded—they say, Check out these transformed entities that never die! All are perversions of the eternality of Christ, and their followers are saying, in effect, "Bite me, so I can live forever!"

This is blasphemy of true communion, when believers feast in faith on the one who bought eternal life. The undead that are dead and buried but crawl out of their graves (a common element in horror movies

177

and the zombie tradition) enact a parody of the resurrection of Christ. The multitudes of young people who follow these genres are saying, "I don't want to be dead. I want to live forever!" Fantasies that follow the Tolkien tradition, in medieval and other dress, attract those who are drawn to—and in some instances repulsed by—the destructive acts of war. I spare gentle readers the usual gore of the worst video games.

The novels *Born Brothers* and *Beyond the Bedroom Wall* and *Poppa John*, deal explicitly with faith. My editor at the house that published them never said, "Larry, you have to cut this religious stuff" or "You can't write openly about God for a secular audience." The editor was, to be explicit, that audience.

All that he worried about and worked on, as any good editor, was getting every sentence sharper and clearer and more precise, closer to a goal I was aiming for (it seems almost absurd to use in this postmodern realm, in the midst of the rubble of deconstruction): a semblance of *the truth*.

As bread is the staff of life, which we learn in a truthful book, so story is the staff of the spirit and mind. The Hebrew Bible relates story after story of Israel's ups and downs on its path to eventual truth. And when Jesus has a telling application to apply he doesn't launch into a fine-tuned theological exposition. He tells a story. "Who is my neighbor?" somebody asks.

"A man was traveling from Jerusalem to Jericho," he begins, and we are inside the story, a metaphor we will not forget, about a person commonly called the Good Samaritan, and at the story's end we come to understand that our neighbor is anybody who is put in our way, in whatever situation we might find them or ourselves, down whichever road we travel.

If you work as a writer or reporter you must meet each person with the grace of openness, as Jesus did, seasoned by compassion, rather than with a preconceived or judgmental outlook. You think you're speaking to an ugly thief or snarling shopping-cart collector when you might be entertaining an angel.

C. S. Lewis wrote in a sermon, "The Weight of Glory,"

> The load, or weight, or burden of my neighbor's glory should be laid daily on my back, a load so heavy only humility can carry it . . . There are no ordinary people. You have never talked to a mere mortal. Nations, cultures, art, civilization—these are mortal and their life is to ours as the life of a gnat. But it is immortals whom we joke with, work with, marry, snub, and exploit—immortal horrors or everlasting splendors.[4]

Don't distort or gloss over what you see. You can't ignore the seamy side of present-day culture, which you're bound to encounter, as you already have. You don't want to present a sanitized, goody-two-shoes version of life if that isn't what you observe. That's not ethically honest. Certain works of fiction, including mine, have been criticized for containing content too forthright for the Christian community, when the criticism is put charitably, but that element I can't ethically change. I've never understood how a writer can depict redemption from sin if the reader doesn't see sin in a character to begin with. No writer would equate a mortal work to the inspired Word of Scripture, the creature grabbing at the Creator—other than bearing an image that's tainted and flawed to begin with and has exuded a further stain of rebellion—and any work I've been able to complete is, I confess, an infinity of distance from Scripture.

That's the exact measure: *infinity* of distance.

Yet in Scripture I find deception and adultery and incest and rape and rebellion and murder and every destructive act I care to imagine, up to a tent stake hammered through the head of a man by a woman who lies to him. All this I receive as instruction, without attributing it to the author, as I take instruction from the spikes driven into skin and flesh, between the bones of the hands of the one lifted up to heal me of the destruction of death.

Do you worry about the ethics of all-nighters?—when you have to hand in a story by a certain date and hour, a deadline? Let me affirm that all writing is against a deadline, whether for a class or the staff of life on your table, or a publication that pays enough to scare you witless, or the end of life. All-nighters are not uncommon to the one who knelt on rock at Gethsemane. You can be sure the Spirit who causes cattle to calve will squeeze from your mind the pooling metaphor of acceptable words to fulfill an assignment or commission in an acceptable time.

Are you blocked?—feel you can't write another word? That means you've reached an ethical juncture you aren't ready to face, or haven't yet resolved, and you're being held from it, because you're not ready to take it on—the sensation of the hand at your chest keeping you from the page you want to fill, from a statement that may, ultimately, be irretrievable or rash or destructive.

So live in trust, which is faith, faith itself the exercise of love—the giving of yourself to another in entire trust. Spend yourself prodigiously in your prose. Carry on the upright accuracy of objective sequence laid out by the one whose hidden attributes, all of which aren't quite apparent in the Word, are visible everywhere in the cosmos. And remind yourself daily, as I must, that the ethics of the life you lead tends to bring you nearer to the truth that you will, more and more, begin setting your stack of stories down within.

18

A TURN IN AESTHETICS
AS A CENTURY TURNS

In the April 16, 2000 issue of the *New York Times* magazine, I came across an article that made me sit up straight. It was titled "Enemies, a Love Story," after the Isaac Singer novel, I assumed. It was written by Andrew Sullivan, a contributing editor at the *Times* who mentions he is gay and HIV positive, and now is a talking head on TV. His article deals with how he came to attend, incognito, the seventieth birthday party for Pat Robertson in the Grand Ballroom of the Washington Hilton.

"I was curious to watch the enemy at ease," he writes.[1] One of his first impressions is of the number of African Americans present. "There were more in the room than there were at the last two events I attended there, the White House Correspondents Dinner and a dinner for Human Rights Campaign, a gay group."[2] Sullivan sits anonymously at a table with a hodgepodge of Christians and finds himself thinking, as he writes in his semieditorial piece, "They were—how can I put this delicately?—charming. They seemed neither fanatics nor bigots. They had a sense of humor about themselves."[3]

When Sullivan mentions to friends how disarmed he was by the evening, they react with alarm. "Some of them viscerally compared the event to a Nazi rally," he writes.[4] But from his actual experience, he encountered no bashing, not even political comment, the entire evening, and he can't merely erase the effects of that, he says, and asks, "To what extent, I wonder, can one attribute good motives to people with whom one deeply disagrees?"[5] After he thinks this and other matters through, such as Robertson's humanitarian efforts, he concludes—and these are his exact concluding sentences, down to the last:

> It's one thing, after all, to be charmed out of your convictions. It's another to keep your convictions and see the motives and conflicts of one's opponents in a more sympathetic light. They are human beings, too. They can crack jokes, forget place cards and wear unforgivable outfits. They can also save lives, feed the poor and treat the sick. If we have come to a point in the culture war where we are too bitter to acknowledge and admire this, then it is time—in fact, it is way past time—for a truce.[6]

I doubt if any journalism I've read in the last decade has had quite the impact on the aesthetic quality of what I write as that. I was in a vulnerable state on April, 16, 2000, but that's not the reason. I had finished a memoir that seemed to disassemble me, in assigning segments of myself to scenes fashioned from words, and on that date in April after taxes are due, I was sitting in the apartment of my son-in-law and daughter, during a breathing space on one of several-city book tours that distress one further—all those talks and interviews providing the opportunity, as I was feeling, for further public disassembly.

It wasn't so much that as a need I felt to return to my first love—the human being, the human condition, the human body, even, in its diversity and flaws and perfections. That was where my attention should be fixed, as it had been, and higher, on the one who, in ways mostly invisible, fixed me.

Then I came across this passage in Marilynne Robinson's collection of essays, *The Death of Adam:*

> It seems to me that when we lost our aesthetic pleasure in the human presence as a thing to be looked at and contemplated, at the same time we ceased to enjoy human act and gesture, which civilization has always before found to be beautiful even when it was also grievous and terrible, as the epics and tragedies and the grandest novels testify. Now when we read history, increasingly we read it as a record of cyni-

cism and manipulation. We assume that nothing is what it appears to be, that it is less and worse, insofar as it might once have seemed worthy of respectful interest. We routinely disqualify testimony that would plead for extenuation. That is, we are so persuaded of the rightness of our judgment as to invalidate evidence that does not confirm us in it. Nothing that deserves to be called truth could ever be arrived at by such means. If truth in this sense is essentially inaccessible in any case, that should only confirm us in humility and awe.[7]

I had become that sort of internal cynic, I saw, and had lost the thread of my aesthetic story.

Aesthetics is about taste, or forming a criticism of taste, which has to do with a sense of the beautiful; it is also a branch of philosophy that establishes a theory of the beautiful, usually pertaining to the fine arts.

A philosopher and aesthetician from Toronto, Calvin Seerveld, in one of his books on aesthetics, *Rainbows for a Fallen World*, says that aesthetics is a branch of philosophy where trained specialists work, but the *practice* of aesthetics is the responsibility of every person in the world, especially those who call themselves Christians. We exercise aesthetic taste by choosing where and how we live, what we surround ourselves with, how we dress, how we talk, what we read, what we eat, and how we spend our leisure time. There is no way we can escape our aesthetic task, Seerveld says.[8]

Which is what few philosophers and scholars are willing to say: that aesthetics is a moral dimension—a decision, sometimes hinging on a single word, of what is good or bad, right or wrong—decisions that arrive from realms superior to one's personal opinion. The British novelist Anthony Burgess, in a textbook he wrote and later revamped, *English Literature: A Survey for Students*, writes at length to elucidate this point:

> "Truth" is a word used in many different ways—"You're not telling the truth." "The truth about conditions in Russia." "Beauty is truth, truth beauty." I want to use it here in the sense of *what lies behind an outward show*. Let me hasten to explain by giving an example. The sun rises in the east and sets in the west. That is what we see; that

is the "outward show." In the past the outward show was regarded as the truth. But then a scientist came along to question it and then to announce that the truth was quite different from the appearance: the truth was that the earth revolved and the sun remained still—the outward show was telling a lie. The curious thing about scientific truths like this is that they often seem so useless. It makes no difference to the average man whether the sun moves or the earth moves. He still has to rise at dawn and stop work at dusk. But because a thing is useless does not mean that it is *valueless*. Scientists still think it worthwhile to pursue truth. They do not expect laws of gravitation and relativity are going to make much difference in everyday life, but they think it is a *valuable* activity to ask their eternal questions about the universe. And so we say that truth—the thing they are looking for—is a *value*.

Truth is one value. Another is beauty. And here, having talked about the scientist, I turn to the artist. The scientist's concern is truth, the artist's concern is beauty. Now some philosophers tell us that beauty and truth are the same thing. They say there is only one value, one eternal thing which we can call *x*, and that truth is the name given to it by the scientist and beauty the name given to it by the artist. Let us try to make this clear. There is a substance called salt. If I am a blind man I have to rely on my sense of taste to describe it: salt to me is a substance with a taste we can only call "salty." If I have my eyesight but no sense of taste I have to describe salt as a white crystalline substance. Now both descriptions are correct, but neither is complete in itself. Each description concentrates on *one way of examining salt*. It is possible to say that the scientist examines *x* in one way, the artist examines it in another. Beauty is one aspect of *x*, truth is another. But what is *x*? Some call it ultimate reality—the thing that is left when the universe of appearances, of outward show, is removed. Other people call it God, and they say beauty and truth are two of the qualities of God.[9]

One of the reasons I lost the thread of my aesthetic story was that whenever I published a book that I thought was fairly beautiful and certainly truthful, but contained Christian content, the literary network that extends from New York outward tended to treat it as unworthy of serious consideration. Or assumed the book was a mere rehash of moral dilemmas already overworked by others with an affinity for the same bypassed religion—surely primitive and provincial, and *therefore*, with nothing to say. The attitude left me feeling like a pre-Sullivan caricature at a Pat Robertson party.

About provincial overworking of primitive material, Katherine Anne Porter says about the work of Willa Cather, who ranks high in my estimation, "Freud had appeared: but Miss Cather continued to cite the old Hebrew prophets, the Greek dramatists, Goethe, Shakespeare, Dante, Tolstoy, Flaubert, and such for the deeper truths of human nature, both good and evil."[10] And Porter mentions the critic Maxwell Geismar, who wrote a book on Cather and others, *The Last of the Provincials*:

> He has a case: she is a provincial; and I hope not the last. She was a good artist, and all true art is provincial in the most realistic sense: of the very time and place of its making, out of human beings who are so particularly limited by their situation, whose faces and names are real and whose lives begin each one at one individual unique center. Indeed, Willa Cather was as provincial as Hawthorne or Flaubert or Turgenev . . . [11]

Fiction containing provincial or primitive Christianity, as judged by perfectionist elites, is often passed over or dismissed, no matter its literary quality or aesthetic level. That tendency, however misguided or prejudicial, can be seen as partly earned. Contemporary Christian fiction often lacks artistic or aesthetically pleasing complexity. It shies from the descriptive detail and truth of Chaucer, Dante, Shakespeare, Donne, or Anne Bradstreet, and most in that tradition, nor is it G. K. Chesterton or Graham Greene or Frederick Buechner or Flannery O'Connor or Marilynne Robinson or the Johns Updike or Cheever—to which some may say, Good, Amen! It doesn't even aspire to that level. It seems unaware of their stories and novels or of any Christian tradition. Marilynne Robinson, who remains true to the Christian truths that astonished her as a child, has on the other hand received wide attention in critical circles, which is deserved—her artistry so consummate the construction of a sentence can send up a sting of tears; however, she remains stubborn as a rusty spike at any attempt to dislodge her convictions.

I was further gawkily lost in 2000, because I was descending to the outlook of my undergraduate years, a state defined in a novel by Robert Pirsig—not *Zen and the Art of Motorcycle Maintenance*, which I appreciate on another level—rather *LILA*, in which he outlines the malady:

> Everyone seemed to be guided by an "objective," "scientific" view of life that told each person that his essential self is his evolved material body. Ideas and societies are a component of brains, not the other way around. No two brains can merge physically, and therefore no two people can ever really communicate except in the mode of ship's radio operators sending messages back and forth in the night. A scientific, intellectual culture had become a culture of millions of isolated people living and dying in little cells of psychic solitary confinement, unable to talk to one another, really, and unable to judge one another because scientifically speaking it is impossible to do so. Each individual in his cell of isolation was told that no matter how hard he tried, no matter how hard he worked, his whole life is that of an animal that lives and dies like any other animal.[12]

This echoes the ironic comment W. H. Auden includes in the poem "In Memory of W. B. Yeats," that "each in the cell of himself is almost convinced of his freedom."[13] Textrs may think they're free of all that but the truth is probably closer to what an undergraduate recently said in a seminar: "Ten years from now we'll have to have classes on how to talk to one another."

My disillusion caused regression to the state Pirsig and Auden describe. I no longer saw myself, and even more relevant, others (if a writer possesses a gift, it's in serving others, if only one's characters) as the crown of creation, as Marilynne Robinson puts it, echoing Psalm Eight. She wrote an essay using "Psalm Eight" as its title, and in that psalm humankind is seen as only a little lower than the angels.

Darwinism had taken me in its down elevator to the state I was in, and I was edging into the culture that tended to debase the Davidic "old Hebrew prophet" and instead went for Goth or punk, the pierced, torn, and tattooed—ripped jeans cinched below hips—partly from the disassembly the memoir brought about. If I seem to protest too much, I've tried to include a counterpoint in a variety of voices and views on this theme. However you take it, I wasn't surviving in the fittest mode.

Marilynne Robinson opened another avenue in *The Death of Adam* when I found "The notion of 'fitness' is not now and never has been value neutral"[14]—any more than critical aesthetics ever are, let me add. She notes that in *The Descent of Man*, Darwin writes, in these exact words,

> With savages, the weak in body or mind are soon eliminated; and those that survive commonly exhibit a vigorous state of health. We civilized men, on the other hand, do our utmost to check the process of elimination; we build asylums for the imbecile, the maimed, and the sick; we institute poor laws; and our medical men exert their utmost skill to save the life of everyone to the last moment… Thus the weak members of civilized society propagate their kind. No one who has attended to the breeding of domestic animals will doubt that this must be highly injurious to the race of man. It is surprising how soon a want of care, or care wrongly directed, leads to the degeneration of a domestic race; but excepting in the case of man himself, hardly anyone is so ignorant as to allow his worst animals to breed.

Robinson adds, "None of this is abstract of general or innocent of political implication. *The Descent of Man* (1871) is a late work which seems to be largely ignored by Darwinists now."[15] And she notes how it bears "mentioning in this context that the full title of Darwin's first book is *On the Origin of Species by Means of Natural Selection, or the Preservation of Favoured Races in the Struggle for Life.*"[16]

Another cultural icon, Sigmund Freud, was influenced by Darwin in several ways, as Robinson illustrates:

> In the *Future of Illusion*, Freud ridicules the idea that one might love one's neighbor as oneself, a commandment Jesus quotes from Leviticus, on the grounds that it is contrary to human nature. This is the great peculiarity of this school of thought, that it wishes to make an ethic of what it presents as an inevitability when, if inevitability were a factor, no ethic would be needed.

Freud's star has dimmed, at last. But his theories . . . are remarkably meager and charmless. Their lack of scientific foundation, their prima facie implausibility, and their profound impact on modern thought, prove together that we can in fact choose myths which will function for us as myths, that is, that will express visions of reality which form values and behavior. This thought is more frightening than reassuring, though if Freud had not been able to adapt the great influence of Darwin and Nietzsche to his purposes, and if they had not themselves been codifiers of widely held attitudes, Freudian theories would never have achieved the status of myth. Since we do in fact have some power of choice, however, what in the world could have moved us to choose anything so graceless and ugly?[17]

How could I, back in the faith of my beginnings, decades older, contemplate descending toward that kind of ugliness again? Was it impatience for attention crossing wires with lack of faith?

In a Lawrence Weschler *New Yorker* profile in the same year of this century's turn, he interviews Mark Salzman about his novel, *Lying Awake* (a nun faces a crisis of faith), and a piece for cello, based on the novel, that Salzman has composed; Salzman says,

"The thing is, I'm agnostic. I was raised in a non-religious family. Before I started the book, pretty much all I knew about Christianity was what I'd learned from Linus on 'A Charlie Brown Christmas.' My character had dedicated her life to living by faith, not reason. Whereas, of course, I live by reason. I'd assumed that such a character would be quite a stretch for me, but that was all right: a good writer welcomes that kind of gulf."

But it turned out that it wasn't that much of a stretch after all, he went on. The artistic wager—the commitment to devote ever-lengthening years of one's life, say, to the production of a novel; the conviction that such a commitment will make any sort of difference to anyone else, is manifestly unreasonable. "I take it on faith that art is worthwhile. I go on because I believe it's the right thing to do, not because I know it is."[18]

Writing moves forward on belief as sure as lived-out faith—that the uprights and loops that form words will extend into sentences to the end of a page and on to another, each page making sense, the whole eventually cohering in a novel—an act of faith few writers confess. Present-day culture tends to reject the idea of a human being as the unique crown of creation, denying in essence that humankind is the single species—to flip the scientific switch—able to exercise faith. Darwin's response to anybody who objected to the idea of being related to a monkey was, Better a monkey than a naked savage from Tierra del Fuego. Is it any wonder that those who study Darwin can trace the descent of his words through Nietzsche to Marx to Hitler's *Mein Kampf* and the extermination of millions by design to purify a "superior" race?

To return to Marilynne Robinson and her essay "Darwinism" from *The Death of Adam*:

> History is a nightmare, generally speaking, and the effect of religion, where its authority has been claimed, has been horrific as well as benign. Even in saying this, however, we are judging history in terms religion has supplied. The proof of this is that in the twentieth century, "scientific" policies of extermination, undertaken in the case of Stalin to purge society of parasitic or degenerate or recalcitrant elements, and in the case of Hitler to purge it of the weak and ineffective or, racially speaking, marginally human, have taken horror to new extremes. Their scale and relentlessness have been owed to the disarming of moral response by theories authorized by the word "science," which, quite inappropriately, has been used as if it meant "truth." Surely it is fair to say that science is to the "science" that inspired exterminations as Christianity is to the "Christianity" that inspired Crusades. In both cases the human genius for finding pretexts seized upon the most prestigious institution of the culture and appropriated a great part of its language and resources and legitimacy. In the case of religion, the best and worst of it have been discredited altogether. In the case of science, neither has been discredited. The failure in both instances to distinguish best from worst means that both science and religion are effectively lost to us in terms of disciplining or enlarging our thinking.
>
> These are not the worst consequences, however. The modern fable is that science exposed religion as a delusion and more or less supplanted it. But science cannot serve in the place of religion because it cannot generate an ethics or a morality. It can give us no reason to prefer a child to a dog, or to choose honorable poverty over fraudulent wealth. It can give us no grounds for preferring what is

excellent to what is sensationalistic. And this is more or less where we are now.[19]

It was indeed where we were as the century turned and it's obvious we're now leagues beyond. But as I underwent an unhappy crumbling with the old century, I was cheered and turned by Andrew Sullivan and so exhilarated by Marilynne Robinson I had to restrain myself from quoting her more—confirmed by their messages of the rightness of the walk I had been displaced from, the beauty of it, the beauties of holiness that settle us a little lower only than the angels.

And yet another *New Yorker* writer, Daphne Merkin, said, "I've been trying to lose my religion for years now, but it refuses to go away . . . You'd think it would be easy, particularly in a city like New York, where no one cares whether or not you believe in God; even my friends who do would be hard put to explain why, other than by alluding knowingly to Pascal's wager, in which the odds favor the believer. But as the world becomes a more bewildering place almost by the week, I find myself longing for what I thought I'd never long for again: a sense of community in the midst of the impersonal vastness, a tribe to call my own."[20]

Where I stand in the tribe I've been called into is best expressed in an aesthetic way, in a thicket as packed and surprising as faith, in "Holy Sonnet XV" by John Donne:

> Wilt thou love God, as he thee! then digest,
> My Soule, this wholesome meditation,
> How God the Spirit, by Angels waited on
> In Heaven, doth make his Temple in thy brest.
> The Father, having begot a Sonne most blest,
> And still begetting, (for he ne'r begonne)
> Hath deign'd to chuse thee by adoption,
> Coheire to'his glory, 'and Sabbaths endlesse rest.
> And as a robb'd man, which by search doth finde
> His stolne stuffe sold, must lose or buy'it againe:
> The Sonne of glory came downe, and was slaine,
> Us whom he'had made, and Satan stolne, to unbinde.
> 'Twas much, that man was made like God before,
> But, that God should be made like man, much more.[21]

19

A FINAL MEETING AT THE ALGONQUIN HOTEL

(reproduced exactly, according to our video-pad transcorder)

"In this season of awards, including this my most recent, thank you, it seems irreverent not to mention the Nobel. Oh, dingee! aware am I of my monumental misstep in mentioning *that* by name (crap), as Newark belletrist Philip Roth, exemplar of timely attitudes, said after, you know, a plaque was fixed to his boyhood home, 'Today, Newark is my Stockholm, and that plaque is my prize.'[1] Writers daren't mention it though eyes bug prize-wise at the thought of a million dollars (before investments!) clattering into one's bank account in reward for an oeuvre or career, if one.

"Uncomely as it may seem, then, in reprehensible taste and the rest, *The Prize* is a topic that serious and other writers return to after the party is done and the girls packing pancake and will be your topic by the time you do your business in bed tonight of sleep—regrets that some, as I hear in my headset, sit three deep in the lobby chairs, too distant from the square set at my round table, but hang in!

"Parameters bracket *Prize* paradigm: as, it is not for any who did not feel the effect of Chekhov at say, six, nor for those who did not read every page of *The Magic Mountain* (by T. Mann, who garnered one), nor for those not enamored of Knut Hamsun (a recipient) for a full

191

year, or any able to mention *only*, *My Antonía* by Willa Cather, who did not garner one, or cannot place Vladimir Nabokov (outré for anti-Freudian naughtiness) except as scriptwriter for Kubrick.

"Most importantly, the Nobel, sorry *Prize*, shall not hang from neck to waist of any who, at any point in her or his career, scribed a piece containing 'louche' or 'incumbent' except to refer to a politician, as in 'the incumbent was louche,' not, 'it became incumbent upon her to be louche,' nor to any who use 'impact' as a verb, as in 'I was impacted by that,' unless 'that' is factual matter lodged in one's colon.

"If you have scribed these, especially the last, you forfeit all right to *The Prize* and stop writing! Those who ignore this caution are beginning to exhibit, unbeknownst to themselves or employers (Microsoft and agencies), a lamentable public disintegration evident in the inability to scribe 'every day' when 'every day' is correct rather than 'everyday.'

"It is also true that, in recent eras, as accountants garnered control over businesses once run by thoughtful tweedy readers, publishing, a movement grows to ban fiction from the *Prize*. This to ingratiate the growing audience, according to accountant's polling, who do not care for fiction, would not be caught dead (as said by some who suffer death in crucial regions) reading it, and want just plain cold facts, Ma'am, no coherence or accuracy or, *help me!*, truth. And finally, as to the 'new' *Prize*, we now know from disclosures at the death of an Academy diehard dedicated to the Prize for Peace, what we down the ladder of literature intuited: *Those Prizes* are not given to honor an awardee but to shame the fool who will never get one, no matter the awardee is not a conservationist or peaceful guy, calling to mind that storied playground apothegm, 'Naw, na-na-na *naw* na!'

"There is a difficulty inherent in the process, however, if the person to be (or not to be) shamed is not cognizant of the passover—critical umbrage meanwhile falling in too generalized injuriousness on others, mostly writers, acutely sensitive and vulnerable, who faithfully follow National Public Radio to discern the proper outlook and then fail to win even a Pushcart!

"Writers are aware of unfair bias, providing *Prize* nominators other than self often—the oddball being neighbor Norway's Knut Hamsun, whose Third Reich affinities remained undisclosed until after, or so an Academy story goes; double for Gunter Grass with his Reich-aligned confession *after* receiving it; and paste tail to Marquez and his dedicated love of Castro, a dictator who treats his servants and dissidents with humanitarian blows.

"Let me illustrate a corrected mishap of comparable magnitude in a tale related by the raconteur and CEO of a noble literary firm, Father Stroud & Guru, also married to society standards, with relatives and informers on most literary committees nameable, now gone, sadly, said personally to me in 1975 that fictionist Mellow was to receive *Prize One* when, with *Humbert's Grit,* he was suspected of Mafia affinities. The fussy litmus of literary politics of the Swedish Academy, above mentioned, could not accept into its century-spanning stainlessness a writer close enough to feel the breath of the Mafia on his neck, or back of it, but as next year rolled round and the main man of the reigning vocal Academy opposition deigned to die and it was clear *Prize One* was destined for Mellow, then, back home, a similar committee noted that Mellow had garnered numberless BNAs but never a Pulltitzer!

"Be honest, let me ask, is it odd, no, worse, to see bigots poisoned against particular writers? So Mellow, maybe the salutary United States recipient, I add, to arrest any expected lava of envy, received the Pulltitzer a month before *The Prize*, omission dashed by swift shift of face.

"Can you imagine how many, even taxi drivers, lust after the *Prize* once they hear, in comparison to the Pulltitzer's puny thousands, a million, minus interest, or have I said that?—huge enough to hold creative effort at a halt. For a further fact we face is the fact that *The Prize* in fact is often dropped on writers despite the fact of decline, if not a fact at rope's end—Mellow one of few who wrote a book, besides quirky ones, once *The Prize* hit. Who *is* Sinclair Lewis?

"An American writer the Academy Swedes might consider is Stephen King, who has the oeuvre, the outpour and popularity comparable to long-ago Will Stradford, not to say a revered last name: King of the Nobel! He has thought his way through with virtuous emasculation: 'I am no one's National Book Award or Pulitzer Prize winner'—best to be modest, even when nominating self—'but I'm serious, all right. If you don't believe anything else, believe this: when I take you by your hand and begin to talk, my friend, I believe every word I say.' This from his earlier book, *Four Past Midnight*, on writing (page 608), not the recent one garnering a prize, but of numinous deliquescence in view of decades past composition—though I note that King's phrase after his colon (the punctuation one) is cribbed from the Russian for some reason ineligible, Count Turgidnev. Double that for Count Tolstop, plus the amusing hysterioso, Christian Dostepyopski.

"Born in 1947, author King displays the scribe-fine detachment of a winner, admitting he can't help 'laughing uncontrollably over some wild and crazy bit of fluff I had just finished churning out. I'm never going to be Reynolds Price or Larry Woiwode—it isn't in me' [note, self-nominees, the humility!] '—but that doesn't mean I don't care as deeply about what I do. I have to do what I *can* do, however—as Nils Lofgren once put it, "I gotta be my dirty self . . . I won't play no jive."'

"Mr. Lofgren is, I suspect, a *Prize* judge, and nominees should quote those. I am past consideration due to toe-injuring novels, if dropped on one—too effete, too inclined to knead into pages past panegyrics while purging lapidary dross and stuff during diligent line-edits, too New Yorkerish and humble.

"So as we gather tonight to celebrate my award, may I quote to those who have won nothing, much less a Nobel, a quip from Will Stradford, an oldie who, born too early, was not eligible: 'Friends, I am but hurt!' Suck succor from the fact that all gathered here are *Non*-Nobels, ranking not only among those mentioned (Chekhov, Nabokov, Dostepyopski, Turgidnev, Tolstop, Cather, Roth, to recap) and most *major* American writers, including Norman Major, but also Gandhi, Colette, Lawrence (D. H. and T. E.), Fitzgerald (several), Lessing, Green, Greene, Auden, Billy Graham, and innumerables neither Latino nor Scandinavian.

"Know that No-bells may devolve on loners in obscure locations, even tea fanciers and past masters of "farm novels," as a scurrilous academic tagged mine, as we saw happen hardly a year ago when a humble young writer known for poetic posts on Facebook and Twitter was only two pages into the first draft of his first novel when he, Shadrack Bhrain Ogama, received *The Prize* I'll now say Nobel-ly.

So I speak shucking glory, in my humble opinion, opting not to enlist siblings or my agent to read pages I wrote while drafting a book for which I expect plenty prizing, my roommate predicts, in order to relate my relished tale of two cities, scribed by nonlaureate of longest standing, Don Opdyk.

"Commenting on the current practice of literary capitals (an infelicitous designation, but you get my drift), he says, or so I recall the comment I can't at the moment quote entirely, difficult as it is for books to reach my height, about a lady from a locale who displays uncanny self-esteem in the company of literary partygoers in the East, the place perhaps Connecticut she is visiting, about her provenance of origin, when author-narrator in a naughty aside says, 'She kept talking about "The Twin Cities" as if people knew which cities she meant.'

"Finally, in conclusion to address my end, thank you for the award from the manufacturers of Gas-Ease pellets, designed to improve gas utilization—they work for me!—and eliminate SUVs. My integrated use of these, over and over, in my latest bio-novel, plus a Hubbard's cupboard of organic produce, garnered me the Aloft Award. So I speak to you from my frangible dirigible above a playing field using yet another marvel, the static-free, scribe-laser-video-pad-broadcaster and detoxifying peace-bander provided by DeNeet Boom Industries of Grand Rapids, whose toll free number is—

"Aieeeeee......."

20

A VIEW ON WRITING
FROM ANOTHER COUNTRY

The World & I:[1] Writers have seen themselves as craftsmen, magicians, professional liars, unacknowledged legislators, prophets, and media stars. How do you see the writer?

Larry Woiwode: As a writer—a person who puts together words in a certain order to make sense. I'm sure that Shakespeare, who knew his history fairly well and was knowledgeable about human nature and turned out plays like any good journeyman, would have been appalled by the questions writers are asked today. Writers aren't shamans and the political statements of most seem the same empty pieties we've been hearing for years, as if they're issued to writers by a central organization like PEN. Earlier, Mailer and Updike were at least original, and often amusing.

W&I: Recognition came to you fairly early in life with *What I'm Going to Do, I Think*, which won the William Faulkner Foundation Award for the best first novel of the year. How old were you then? Did the early recognition present problems for you?

LW: I was twenty-seven when the novel came out. It got a lot of critical attention and was a best-seller for a while. Five years before that, I began selling stories to the *New Yorker* and they'd been appearing since, so it wasn't as if I came out of nowhere or was dazzled to see myself in print. But I suspect the attention my first novel received put pressure on the next, *Beyond the Bedroom Wall*. I had also become a father, and one always has to sort the balance between family and writing. I was about to let *Bedroom Wall* go in 1971, two years after the first novel, when my wife Carole said, "What about those earlier generations you always talked about?" So it took another four years to include them and restructure and rewrite the rest. It was rough going at times, yes, although I wasn't often frozen or devastated, and it turned out to be a big book, equal to three or four usual novels in volume—as *Born Brothers* is—so it kept me busy.

W&I: You are an accomplished poet as well as a fiction writer. We pay so little attention to the poet these days. Why is that?

LW: I wanted to be a poet, but I also wanted to make a living as a writer. Was it the advent of interviews, where poets are treated as shamans and gurus that generated impatience in them for the craft? I've observed this impatience in young writers who seem to want to first set the world on its ear and then declaim to its underlings, as it were. Real poetry demands good readers and I believe television has plopped so many down in a stupor there aren't many readers left.

W&I: Much of modern and contemporary fiction concentrates on psychological disintegration. In *Poppa John*, the main character, Ned, goes through a psychic unraveling and so does the narrator of *Born Brothers*, Charles. Why do you think times of acute mental crisis are important to our culture?

LW: Moments of mental crisis are important to the individual, though I would hope individuals in some cultures might learn from the crises some of my characters undergo. Walker Percy says that in the best fictional characters the potential for hope and catastrophe has become escalated, and he has something there. That's why writers focus on such moments. One must also have drama and some sort of decline or rise. That these crises are viewed by many as strictly psychological is, I believe, one of the failures of modern writing and of critics of that writing. Perhaps the crises should be viewed as spiritual deadlocks or problems reflecting the spiritual decline in our culture—anyway, I would like to see more flexibility of possibility and interpretation.

W&I: You are living and teaching in England right now. How do you like it? Do you miss your native North Dakota?

LW: I enjoy the antiquity of England, with the potential for history on every corner. The two-hundred-some years of American history are set in perspective when you realize it took four hundred years to build Canterbury Cathedral, a work undertaken explicitly "to the glory of God" and the work was begun centuries before. On the other hand, I'm irritated by the general hostility to Americans, especially since the goals of most Londoners seem to out-American Americans. It's as if the British, like the Chinese, have been roused from a centuries-long sleep to the possibility of free-market capitalism, and both admire and resent what America has achieved.

W&I: The sense of place plays such an important part in *Born Brothers*—North Dakota might almost be said to be a main character. Would you like to talk about how someone's sense of place relates to his identity?

LW: What about New York City and Illinois in *Born Brothers*, or that cell of a city room where the narrator is stuck? I say to student writers that every character has to have somewhere to walk or sit, and in that sense, setting, or place, is essential. When in our development we learn to walk, we travel over a particular patch of ground, and it seems that its composition—its makeup, layout, geography—has some special effect on us. A child doesn't tend to form opinions until an adult instructs the child how to, and I think we receive the setting of our earliest years with an original and unclouded impact. Other places are in a sense measured against the place where we grew up, for better or worse. I was

born in North Dakota and lived there until I was eight, so by the time I
was a teenager I felt I had grown away from it, and perhaps I had. Out
of college, I moved to New York City and there I found I was writing
about North Dakota. Over the years I was working on *Bedroom Wall*,
North Dakota grew so mythical in my own mind I had to go back and
see whether it was really there, that is, existed in the terms I had imagined. Partly so and partly not, as these things go, but a certain frontier
element I sensed had a further effect on me. So a few years later when
Carole and I started looking in the West for a place to live—we had decided from our years in the East that the East wasn't for us—we found
that one of the few places that hadn't been affected by either coast was
North Dakota.

We moved there and perhaps the move back set the years of my life
inside a kind of parenthesis. Whatever happened, I think a writer can
write with authority only about what he knows, and by now I know
North Dakota fairly well. Carole and our children love it, which always
surprises me, and I've begun to feel at home there—which might say
as much as anything about its relationship to my identity. Yes, I miss it.

W&I: Reading *Born Brothers*, I have the strong suspicion as I feel most
readers will, that the fiction has been built up from a substratum of autobiographical material. Philip Roth has said that the autobiographical
elements of his work, "hooks into reality," help him judge the credit-
ability of the elements in his work which are purely invented. How do
the autobiographical elements relate to the invented elements in your
fiction?

LW: Yes, but . . . whenever "Is this autobiographical" comes up, I sense
the unstated question is, Can this guy write only about himself or does
he have the imagination and intelligence to invent? Present company
excepted, of course. It's somewhat like chess, where you think you
know all the moves and gambits and may have studied matches of the
grand masters, but once you sit down to a game, something happens
that changes the entire atmosphere, and you have to go by the seat of

your pants. I intend to set down an "actual" scene, you might say, or one true to my life, and when a certain amount of words are in place, boom, everything changes and it takes on its own life and meaning and moves into a dimension I'm seeing from the inside. There's certainly truth in what Roth says. I often measure my characters or their actions by what I was doing at their age, unless they're much older, of course, and Saul Bellow says somewhere that whenever a writer thinks he's being least autobiographical, he's being more so. "This isn't me," the writer thinks, his defenses fall, and his writing releases more inner autobiography than passages in somebody like Roth, who pins a good deal of his fiction to actual events, and so is kept on his toes. A writer has to give himself over to his work however he can and the slant of my involvement with characters—I wear them on my shoulders and consciousness—can take on an autobiographical cast, sure. You should understand, too, that there's a certain delight in making a reader think, This must be the way it happened or, perhaps more pointed, This is exactly the way it happened to this guy. But that's the grand and magical cloak of art, the professional lie you mentioned, an effect that gives writers consummate satisfaction. If this draws you further into the work, to imagine it's me, fine.

W&I: *Beyond the Bedroom Wall* and *Born Brothers* both take up the Neumiller family as their subject. *Beyond the Bedroom Wall* gives us "snapshots" of the Neumillers through four generations. *Born Brothers* deals with the last two generations of the Neumillers whom we meet in *Beyond the Bedroom Wall* and begins to acquaint us with a fifth generation. So in *Born Brothers* we have part of the Neumillers' history recapitulated and even some of the same incidents we learned of in *Beyond the Bedroom Wall* narrated again from a different point of view. How do you think of the relationship of the two books? Were there any models you had in mind?

LW: *Born Brothers* is the second novel I started writing and the first I really got going on, the other now gone. The act of getting it down led to a certain character I felt I should write about separately. I did, and that was the first story the *New Yorker* took. I wrote further separate stories about this family, later the Neumillers, and eventually saw that I might be able to put together a generational book I had before only visualized. The work on it eventually drew me out of what is now *Born Brothers* into *Bedroom Wall*.

In the midst of writing that book I accumulated so much material and saw so many possibilities in the Neumiller and Jones families that I sat down and sketched out five books. Then I finished *Beyond the Bedroom Wall* and now I've finished *Born Brothers*, with a couple of other books between, and sometime I hope to get to the others I once saw. They're part of an interrelated series, and I see them as separate spheres of a minigalaxy. The two finished so far are related in this way but it will take the other three to render them the full gravitational weight in their separate orbits. I don't think I had any particular models in mind, though at one point Tolstoy's *War and Peace* encouraged me in the project's possibility, and at another point several Balzac novels helped me see the possible interrelationship between several books. I was drawn early on to Colette's interrelated stories and sketches about her family, and like them a lot.

W&I: If you wrote *Born Brothers* over the course of that many years, how did the vision change for the book through time, and what difficulties did this present in shaping the material?

LW: The overall plan for the books remained approximately the same—perhaps I'm inflexible, or else deluding myself—and I would say about three-fifths of *Born Brothers* went the way I expected it would, except for material I left behind in that early draft I got going on, because it didn't fit, along with the unexpected surprises one is always grateful for. It went pretty much the way I had originally seen it and, indeed, written quite a bit of it, although I had to put it aside for a while to come closer to the language I was hearing in North Dakota. By the time I came to its end, I had twice the material I needed and I had learned, I hope, along the way. A cutting and revamping at that point removed some subtleties or nuances I miss, but allowed the story to stand out clearer, I believe. The concluding poem was there from the start.

W&I: *Beyond the Bedroom Wall* and *Born Brothers* bring alive the world of childhood with an extraordinary vivacity. When we think of a writer to whom childhood is particularly important we think most often of the Romantics. Yet your viewpoint seems quite different from theirs. Could you talk about the importance childhood has for you as a writer?

LW: The Romantic era, with its emphasis on the "I" seems at the root of contemporary problems. Did I want to suggest that? Look at the childish clamoring of the "me generation," which elevated *Looking Out for Number One* to best-sellerdom. I believe I understand Wordsworth when he says "The child is father of the man" if by that he means what I've mentioned—that children take in the world without coloring or prejudging it. The child would be more open and original than his mature self, then, in the matter of perception anyway—that eidetic memory of a child. The trouble with many modern adjudicators is they seem to want to apply the statement backward; they want a child to become "socialized," to conform to his or her "peer group"—offensive jargon—which inhibits exactly what Wordsworth is extolling, while the adjudicators, adults who don't understand children, at the same time agitate for their own autonomy, and the form it takes is a kind of childish free-for-all. Children are obliged to take in all they see as they see it. Sometimes they feel responsible for it. Usually they wonder why it is as it is. What I hope *Born Brothers* is up to, in its emphasis on childhood, is conveying the kind of grief children feel at the inconsistencies of adults. I also hope the book shows the progress of two adults, drawing on the originality of their childhood. There's no doubt that at the conclusion one of the brothers is broken, but that scene is a-chronological—we see him in settled scenes with his son, earlier, at phases of his son's growing up.

W&I: An important theme in *Born Brothers* is memory. The book, at times, seems to consider memory in the way the ancients did when they thought of it as having extensions into eternity. How do you think of the relationship between memory and imagination?

LW: Memory releases imagination into timelessness. Words of truth are immortal. Imagination *is* memory, Nabokov says. If we have no memory, pictorial, verbal, or otherwise, imagination has no ground to rise from. Just as there has to be a child of some sort before you have an adult, there has to be memory for imagination to exist. The adult provides direction and focus and form to the purity of vision and original perception of the child, and imagination, covering all quarters of memory, provides the same form and direction in a work of fiction. Within one mind, events are simultaneous, which is a taste of eternity. I hoped to try to dramatize that.

W&I: The Neumillers are Roman Catholic and then, at the latest point in time in which we see him, Charles Neumiller, the narrator of *Born Brothers*, has become a Presbyterian. This brings into the text a certain amount of what Flannery O'Connor called "the language of piety." The narrator usually takes up this language with a certain degree of self-consciousness, which seems to me an indication of the difficulties involved in using this language. Could you give us your thoughts on the problems in using the language of piety?

LW: In most of the later incarnations of Charles, yes, the Presbyterianism is so, but couldn't one call it the language of celebration? I'm not sure Charles takes that up any more self-consciously than he does acting or entries in his journal or the language of poetry—all present. I consciously chose to have him enter most every event in the novel, as each passage of prose is, in a way, self-consciously entered. He's the narrator. Somewhere along the way I decided this self-consciousness in Charles, reflecting the general malaise I've mentioned, is his greatest problem. Is it that the language of piety expresses what the apostle Paul calls "the offense of the cross"?[2] I don't feel I should limit any type of language, as long as it's artful and apt and rightly used by a character. I know people who, merely hearing the word "Jesus" turn red in fury from the neck up. Humankind, which cannot bear very much *reality*, hates ultimate truth, God's realm. I do. Perhaps we're all self-conscious about that.

W&I: The terror of the bomb gives an apocalyptic cast to the characters expectation in *Born Brothers*. Like your characters, our preoccupation with this potential cataclysm seems to be more than just a part of our desire to survive. What does our dwelling on the end of civilization say about us?

LW: On the simplest level, we're scared. For some that cataclysm is finances. I think that most of us, no matter how we might disguise it at times, feel we'll eventually have to face a reckoning for our actions. I still hear people say, about something regrettable they've done, "I'm going to pay for that!" Dwelling on civilization's end seems less a death wish than fear of an ultimate reckoning. Certain basic intimations or understandings, once they're written on the heart, to use some of that language you mention, can't be washed away even by decades of media propaganda.

W&I: The limits of television come in for a good whacking in *Poppa John* and elsewhere. Do you really think television is a destructive influence in our culture?

LW: Absolutely. Anybody who doesn't has been out of touch for decades. I grew up with television and early on sensed its addictive potential. When Carole and I got married, neither was interested in it. We both read. We never got a TV and after we had children, we didn't want one. There's a tube, a telly, in the London flat we're living in, and in a kind of experiment I've been watching it again. I might say that the British version is tamer than the American, judging from what I catch now and then at Super-8s and the like—except for the BBC using Noam Chomsky as their commentator on American news and politics—but I can safely say that over the years the medium has gotten worse than I could imagine. The documentation on merely its physical effects, especially on children, is so readily available as to suggest no concerned parent would allow one in the house, if they weren't hooked themselves. It makes no difference what I or anybody else says, though, because we're talking about the cow more holy in American culture than religion. Television is the new religion, not to be knocked like the preachers who appear on it.

W&I: Recently, concern has been expressed, most often in connection with the literary "brat pack" that much of contemporary fiction is trivial. Do you think it is?

LW: Our culture runs on trivia. It seems the brat-pack style of fiction is fostered mostly by one man who champions its practitioners and appears to favor the style himself, when he rolls up his sleeves and plunges into his own fiction. Perhaps as readers we've got our just desserts after years of reliance on television—a minimal, nondimensional, bleached, verbal TV.

W&I: Are there cultural factors which make certain times propitious for the production of great literature?

LW: I don't think so. It happens across the centuries out of all sorts of contexts. I don't think it's clear, for instance, whether the age of Elizabeth I gave rise to the great literature we associate with it or whether the literature, seen in retrospect, doesn't add luster to Elizabeth's era. She was a rather autocratic monarch whose inability to make decisions mostly kept her out of trouble. Again, because of television, people nowadays seem to resent complexity, and complexity is the power behind allusive metaphor and all outstanding fiction.

W&I: "Where there is no vision, the people perish," say the Scriptures.[3] If much of our literature is trivial, what needs to change in order for it to thrive once more?

LW: The vision mentioned, as you find it in Proverbs and many variations elsewhere, refers, I think, to the hope of the Messiah—focus on that. It's an inspired prophetic vision, and I think writers have to be careful not to see themselves as prophets of God. They can be *seers*, I believe, and people can indeed perish without the vision you mention, and do. Good writing can help lead some toward that vision, perhaps, or permit them to see portions of it embodied in fictional characters. We need everyday vision, too, yes.

W&I: Not too long ago the critic Richard Gilman gave his opinion that the "Catholic novel" and, indeed, fiction with a religious vision in general, was a phenomenon passing from the literary scene. Do you agree with his assessment?

LW: Now that the novel is dead, variations of it are dying further? What's he been reading—any Walker Percy, J. F. Powers, Mary Gordon? Actually, that seems a pretty autocratic statement, if not prejudicial—like saying "The American Jewish novel is irrelevant." I've just served a five-year term in the academy, and I'm disturbed by the view it takes of Christianity. I've encountered outright rude dismissal and open hostility. There are wonderful exceptions, of course, and one is even more grateful for them, given the milieu, but this is the prevailing trend. You see it reflected in critical theory and criticism—tear apart the logocentric narrative!—and even book reviews, down to the popular media, where the most violent and radical practitioners of Islam are lumped, along with any American who opens the Bible, as "fundamentalists." The great failure of the academy is that no attempt has been made to examine this group, though it keeps growing and gaining adherents, or even to carry on discourse with it. It's perhaps symptomatic of the times that so many millions of such diverse backgrounds can be so summarily dismissed by the academy with such contempt.

W&I: You seem to be a writer with spiritual concerns. What role do you think fiction can play in teaching us about the central religious questions?

LW: I don't just have spiritual concerns, I'd likely be lumped among the many millions under the label of fundamentalist because I have some knowledge of the Bible. In the past few years I've witnessed or experienced prejudice to such a degree I'm concerned for my children. I'm concerned for the freedoms I've taken for granted in the United States—which was founded by sects of believers after they'd helped neutralize the tyrannical rule of royalty in Western Europe. Fiction is a continuing spiritual exercise that any reader may join in on.

W&I: We have talked about your being a writer with spiritual concerns, but you also have a fine sense of the erotic. There is even an ample amount of rambunctious bawdiness in the fiction. How do these things relate to one another?

LW: One to one. C. S. Lewis said that one of the greatest gifts given to the human creature was the mind, but you can't carry it around in a handbasket, and so another necessary gift is the body. I'm not going to check but I suspect I'd find more references in the Scriptures and by Jesus himself to the body than to the mind. Why be a nihilist and espouse those bleak views that have become so commonplace they're the new sentimentality? Life is to be enjoyed, reveled and gloried in out of eternal gratitude, and my characters reflect that in various ways. "Make a joyful noise to the Lord!" one might say, while another produces a sound some secular prudes might find offensive.[4] I'm not purposely trying to be bawdy, but to represent the diversity I see in the world. King David danced and leapt so high in front of the Ark of the Covenant, it seems with no pants on, that his wife was offended, and for that *she* was struck barren. There's enough sanitized misrepresentation of life available for those who go for that and more sex of the sort that should truly offend on daily TV than in my fiction.

W&I: What's ahead for you as a writer?

LW: More books, I hope, if I'm given time by my Creator and Author.

21

A WRITER'S FEEL OF INTERNAL BLEEDING, A TO Z

a.

I was sleeping on the subway the night the cross-town shuttle caught on fire. Forty-Second Street sank two feet and had to be cordoned off. My sleep was from too much beer and I woke at the end of the line, in the Far Rockaways, and found that my guitar, which had been lying on the seat beside me, was gone, stolen. I was so alarmed I decided to see William Maxwell.

I met him a year before, at the University of Illinois, his alma mater, when he came to deliver a lecture titled "The Autobiographical Novelist." A professor who directed me in theater plays, Dr. Charles Shattuck, a friend from Maxwell's college years, took me for coffee with Maxwell and said, "Here's a writer I want you to meet, and Maxwell said, "When you get to New York, come and see me."

I was in New York because of his statement, leaving behind a young woman I hoped to marry, but so far I was afraid to contact Maxwell.

b.

At the *New Yorker* building, on 20 West Forty-Third, I should take the elevator to the twentieth floor, he tells me over the phone, but when the doors part I'm sure I've gone wrong. I'm not at an elegant magazine but in a bare corridor on an abandoned floor, or so it looks—institutional green with dark scuffed battleship linoleum. Then Maxwell comes through a door opening on a dull hall, in a suit and tie, and leads me down a dim passage to his office: a table to the left inside the door, a schoolteacher's desk ahead, and beside it, against the wall to the right, a cream-colored couch whose fabric looks like patterned silk.

Past the table to the left are windows with low sills. I go to one, partly blinded by the light at this level, and find I'm facing north—Central Park in a green swoon far below.

He steps up close, also looking out. "What do you think of the view?" His words feel so fraught with literary overtones I can't speak.

He asks if I received the letter he sent to Urbana, and I say no. It must have arrived about the time I left, he says, and was meant to let me know the poems I sent to him were with Howard Moss, the poetry editor, but Moss has been ill.

He draws an oak chair from the table and revolves it toward his desk and by the time I sit he's in his swivel chair, hands clasped behind his head, elbows out.

"Will you be able to manage alone in the city?"

"Yes." Though the reason I've worked up courage to see him is to ask for a job at the magazine.

"In my letter I gave what I called Ciceronian advice. That awful Walt-Disneyish World's Fair may result in a kind of mass irritability, I said, which would not be helpful if you're looking for a job."

I flinch at his reading of my mind.

"So from that point of view I thought it might be worth it for you to think of not coming till fall. But I don't really know there will be irritability or that it will affect things for you one way or another. Maybe we had a glimpse of that last night. Did you know the shuttle from Times Square to Grand Central went up in flames?"

"Yes."

"Anyway, you're at the stage of your life where every action, looked back on later, proves to have been destined, so whatever you do don't listen to advice from middle-aged people like me. Here in the city, your story will walk up to you."

c.

Outside, in Times Square, the story walks up in the form of Jude, from our theater group at Illinois, a young woman with the aged and confused aspect of a character actress. She says a friend of a friend needs somebody for a play at Hunter College, and as we talk, she says "Come along" and leads me to the Overseas Press Club, across from Bryant Park, where we take an elevator up and walk to a door with "Attention, Inc." taped across it—a PR mailing firm with rooms so small its offset press sits over the tub in a bathroom and discarded printed pages rise to the faucets like novels gone astray, awry, awash.

The help is mostly unemployed actors—Jude works there; she was on her lunch break—and one of the owners, Van Varner, says, "Come and go as you please, keep your own time," while typewriters clack and the press above the bathtub echoes ka-*thock*, ka-*thock!* against the bathroom walls.

The job is enough for food and a room on St. Mark's Place—a Ukrainian and Puerto Rican neighborhood with older Italian families moving out, not the fashionable place it will become. I promised to allot myself a year to write but give in to Jude's friend who is looking for somebody to fill out her cast. She needs one more to make up a three-character show, a recent translation of a German expressionist drama, *Three Blind Men*.

The three of us rehearse in a bare room, eyes shut from day one, groping our way through her blocking. I don't care for the play and regret abandoning my plans—a vow not to step onstage till a year of writing was up—and on weekends, guilty, I drink too much, back from rehearsals.

d.

April, 1964: Time moves only as counterpoint to the isolated mind, I wrote in the notebook I kept then. *And her inflections in time, her grace notes ad infinitum, were no longer great enough to touch him.*

Which was a way of saying it was not *her*, the young woman I hoped to marry, I missed, but— Well, of course it was.

e.

A week after I start work at Attention they move to Lex and Thirty-Fourth, a second-floor-through in a squat building. Jude gives me the number of a grad student from Illinois finishing his doctorate in the city, and he says with a sigh, in an accent developed after a year in England, "Come over and I'll help you put together a résumé. That way you can, well, get a *real* job."

He lives on Pineapple Street in Brooklyn Heights, down from the St. George, an upscale neighborhood, I see, as I scout around before going up.

We put together a résumé he feels will gain me entrée to literary agencies, where I can work as a reader, and suggests I first try Sterling Lord. I carry my résumé up and *have a seat*, as I'm told, and page through a file folder of poems and writing samples, in case I'm asked. After an hour I'm ushered into the office of a kindly looking, older, urbane gentleman.

"I had to look at the guy who's passing this," he says, and shakes the résumé at me. "Where did you get this?"

"I typed it up at a friend's and had another friend run it off at the place where I work."

"Inventive, eh?"

"Inventive?"

"Nobody could do this much by age twenty-two. Don't give me that. Go on, get out of here!"

We left out a number of the entries as we put together the résumé, and Lord's was the only agency that would grant me an interview.

f.

July, 1964: It's difficult to change the character under whose identity you first meet someone. If you were grave in their presence the first meeting, you will continue to be grave. If you were clownish, you know they expect that from you, and will be a clown. Of course you'll feel other emotions but they'll all be under the auspices of the dominant one you exposed that first meeting.

g.

I'm out of money, except for the few hours a week I work at Attention, worse off than a student. I send a note asking to see Maxwell and hear right back, "I'm running off schedule this week, and you might not find me in. If your job permits it, would you like to have a quick lunch with me this coming Thursday? If you could be at the office at 12:30 that would be best for me."

"Going to see Maxwell again?" Van Varner asks. His favorite writers are Hortense Calisher and Muriel Spark, he says, but he knows Maxwell's novels and stories, and has met him. "I live down the block from Howard Moss," he said once. "Edward Albee is a neighbor." He puts on a prim face of fake concern. "I'm a kind of writer, too, you know!"

He is so energetic jumpiness overtakes him. "How now!" he'll cry, and spin to the postage meter, feeding a stack of letters through, baring his teeth in a fixed grin, jerking glances at the unemployed actors sitting around in their depressed state. His red-sandy hair, like his exuberance going up in flame, is erratically mussed, his tie looks stuffed or crooked in his loosely bulging button-down collar or drags over one side of his shoulder from his hurry—now tapping first one foot then the other as he works the postage meter, his pouter-pigeon chest pulling at the buttons of his shirt.

"Yes, I write!" he adds generally for anybody who might be listening. "I do, I do! For *Guideposts*! The truthful little mag of everyday hope!"

Attention handles *Guideposts'* publicity mailing and manages their exhibit at the World's Fair, and Van is indeed on the staff, a contributing editor. The World's Fair, in distant Queens beside the gaudy stadium of the comic team meant to compensate for the loss of the Dodgers, is not that disruptive, contra Maxwell's fears, as I find one weekend when

I take the subway out to deliver brochures. I'm greeted by Norman Vincent Peale, a cherubic version of the photo of Oswald Spengler on *The Decline of the West*, one of my inamorata's favorite books, often in her arms when we walked together at Urbana, along with Theodore Reik's *Of Love and Lust*.

h.

The daughter of Leonard LeSourd, editor of *Guideposts* and second spouse of Katherine Marshall, the wife of the Marshall of *A Man Called Peter*, works at Attention that summer, occasionally manning the *Guideposts* counter in the Billy Graham pavilion, a dark beauty with a settled regard on a realm greater than herself, able to look straight at you but not with the look that invites you in, and can swing her body toward you, with plenty to swing, without offering it. I'm able to talk to her only in the joking banter of Van, aware she's unapproachable by such pig claws as I carry, or so I recognize in the present, and never did press an approach, thank God.

i.

Maxwell and I descend in an elevator from his office and he hails a cab and says, "Fifty-Ninth at this corner of the Park." He carries a brown paper bag and we sit on a bench up a slope from the lagoon and eat chicken wrapped in wax paper, as if prepared at home. I gulp mine, so desperate to tell him I need a job I find I can't talk. He mentions writers he believes I should read, and I miss one or two, crammed so full of the question I'm trying to ask. Soon we're in a cab and back up the elevator to his office and he's staring at me, hands clasped behind his neck. I tell him I'm trying to write a story, but—

"Good. Whatever you want with your whole heart to do, you will. Chuck Shattuck says you're a writer, and I'm sure you're the kind only you can be. It's written all over your face. It's the half-formed and half-hearted desires and ambitions that go unrealized. But you know what you want, and that's how it will turn out for you. No force in the world, no person living or dead, can alter that.

"If I seem to be meddling too much, you have to say so. You have to make allowance for my concern for people—that they are not cold, that they are not hungry, that they have a roof over their head, that they don't have to bear alone a terrible weight on their heart, and on and on. I can meddle in that way and you'll have to tell me when to stop because I do not in any way want to come between you and your will to be a writer. Do you have money enough to live on?"

"Yes." It shames me to think I was planning to ask for a job when by his word he has defined me as a writer.

j.

July: I believe I have found an important part of my subject matter in the use of actors and theater. My concern for the real over the artificial, the symbolic over the formless, the eternal over man, has, with this subject matter, a tremendous opportunity to speak without seeming contrived or didactic. Besides, I am theater.

Aug, 22, 1964: Let me, then, for interest and for future reference, put down my expenses . . .

.70 for a "Hamburger Plate," heaped with fries and with a thimble of slaw and a coke.

.25—tip for the waiter

.35—a pack of cigarettes (Tareytons: "I'd rather fight than switch")

.20—ice cream cone (black raspberry)

1.00—to a beggar, the same one (and I'm not letting my need for penance sway me) I passed up several days ago. Now he is near death. He can only talk in a breathless rasp, has hardly any coordination (he sat all the time I talked to him) and is nearly blind. He is dirtier now and his sooty face is streaked with tears. His last words, "I'll say a prayer for you, I will. Excuse me, I can't talk"—holding his throat with his hand—"I'll say a prayer for you."

"Please do."

What made him so breakable, broken?

k.

Some weekends I hand all my money to street people and have to walk to Attention, weak-legged and trembling from hunger, and usually on those days, near noon, the other partner at Attention, Harold, will step into the back room and say, "Who wants to get us burgers from Prexy's?"—a joint down the street—"I'm buying." Harold is chief typist-typesetter for the offset press run by Don, who is from Brooklyn and has a gift of mimicry and memory that enables him to reel off dozens of Burns' poems in a Scots brogue, although he isn't one of the unemployed actors. He's better.

l.

At the end of a penniless day I have to ask for a cash advance from Austra-at-the-front-desk, a purse keeper who is scrupulous never to lend as much as I earned the week before. She is executive and receptionist and secretary and gatekeeper, a single and saintly woman who might have been a nun but turned herself over to Van and Harold, or rather to their business, as their servant. Both are bright but don't have an organizational business sense. Van goes dancing off on creative flights and Harold, who can rattle away on a Selectric at eighty words a minute, a graduate of Pace, is a task finisher. His wife, who appears in the office wheeling a baby stroller, with another child walking beside, gripping its rail, has a severe look but in conversation is gracious, solicitous, and I imagine it is her money that funds Attention and keeps her face in its concentrated grip.

She speaks mostly to Austra and Harold.

m.

I finish a story, "Five Letters," about the letters a character reads and responds to over one night, with interspersed passages that tell a different back story and contradict the letters, Gide-like, I think, and deliver the story to Maxwell. I've mentioned Andre Gide before—my fascination with the *Journals*. He asks if I've read Colette, then brings me up to date on the difficulties-of-learning-to-play-the-piano-after-fifty, as he's been trying to do and has talked about before, and then says, "I looked at Gide's *Journals* and the more I hear about his piano playing the more I'm led to believe he could barely play a lick on it and was making half that up."

I feel the heat of this and he looks startled, his lips parted, and then we start laughing at the same moment—Maxwell with gleeful seizures that it seems he finds it difficult to get to stop.

"Have you read *Rabbit, Run?*" he asks, wiping at the corner of each eye with a little finger. I started it once, I say, but at the time— He takes me down to a bookstore on the street and puts a copy in my hand.

Next week the volume of *My Mother's House and Sido*, pulled from his library, arrives in the mail, with a note saying this is closer to what I do. I'm so taken by Colette I'm reluctant to return the book and when I do he says, as if he's read me out again, "No, keep it. I intended it for you."

n.

Aug 11, St. Marks: Absurd as it may sound, I believe that the isolation of my protagonists in a high place (attic, hay mow, five-story room) is an expression of their desire to get nearer a mystic source: God, if you will.

The temptation of large, rococo words. Shun everything that is not precise, honest, and unobtrusive. Allow the thought to carry the words with it; don't limit it with rhetoric or pedantry. I write all this tonight in haste, guilty that I didn't keep at my story.

o.

In this story I include Shattuck and a writing instructor melded into one character, Serafim, and *her* and my parents and more, pouring material for two novels into it. I ask Van's permission to stay at Attention after hours, to use one of their Selectrics to type it up, and feel such exhaustion at morning light I lie on a piece of cardboard in the press room, and wake to screaming. Austra has come in early and seen my legs and is sure a vagrant has broken into the offices and died.

Van asks me to stay after work and I think, *This is it.*

When everybody is gone from the office he grabs a sheaf of typed pages and does a dance to the sorting table where I sit.

"Will you help me with this?" he asks.

It's a first-person piece for *Guideposts*, about a young man who returns home and "for the first time" recognizes the worth of his parents; it isn't bad, as far as it goes, the writing is clear, and I'm pleased he has asked me to help. "Is this about you? Are you from Kansas?"

"Oh, no! I'm a *Suthen* boy. Vah*gin*ya."

"What I'm reading never happened?"

"Well, *kind* of. We don't always get such wonderful stories and have to rewrite or fill in with our own. You know about editors and *quality*, no? What do you think?"

"It's not bad."

"Not a little forced at the end when I use italics?"

"I was going to say you should drop those and simplify the language right there, so it's more like the character's thoughts at that age. Then it'll be better."

"Thank you. *Thank* you!" He grasps the sides of my head in his hands and kisses my hair. "If there is ever any favor I can do, ask, even to staying in my extraordinary bachelor's pad, if you like—while I'm on vacation, of course. Usually in July, by the way."

p.

I do not wonder whether he's gay, nor is that a criterion of judgment, after working with theater people for years when "gay" was recherché and they were generally more circumspect in their approach (partly because of the era, perhaps) than the Don Juans and sybarites.

q.

On a visit to deliver "Five Letters" I learn from Maxwell that he worked with Nabokov on *The Defense*—appearing that month in episodes in the magazine—and Nabokov, for me, is the hottest thing since fry bread, so "What did he *say*?" I ask.

"I hardly remember. It was one of those talks where with not so many words you seem to follow what the other is saying. After the work on proofs I walked him back to his hotel and he asked me up and I sat in a chair with my coat on. He was lying on his hotel bedcovers in his suit and shoes with his head on a pillow and his hands clasped under his head. Oh, one thing that should amuse you; he said that for too long he labored under the misconception that a writer of his stature had to screw everything in sight and nearly lost his wife that way."

I take this as a rebuke, as I gradually move into illumination over an earlier statement of his: "I've come to believe young men in New York tend to employ women for entirely sanitary reasons." When it's obvious this has sailed past me, he adds, "To keep from dirtying their personal bed linen."

r.

Sept 21, 1964: No entries now for over a week. Deep in the transition state—the change Maxwell saw in me three weeks ago.

s.

Sept 24, 2 a.m.: Tuesday, yesterday, Maxwell received my letter and called right away, asking me to come either for lunch or at 4:00. I don't know why I chose four; I hadn't eaten and didn't have any money. He wanted to see me because of a paragraph in my letter,

> *I think I've ruined most of my fiction. Instead of being honest I've been trying to be profound. It's impossible to be profound if you're not. Besides, it seems as soon as you try to be profound about people, since they are what writing is about, you miss all their humanity.*

t.

He was overjoyed to hear "the good news" . . .

U.

He wants me to write a factual account of the last week, and I've been cursing myself for not keeping this notebook. He wants me to write simple exercises, "Just for me, without any thought of publication."

V.

Maxwell and I call the pages he believes will be my first novel "My Brother's Visit to New York." I look at *New Yorkers* on newsstands or buy issues when I can, and it seems a story I wrote in a rush at Urbana comes closest to what I'm reading, "Requiem and Fall." I prune out the worst literary passages, which I'm learning to identify, retype it, and address it to Mr. William Maxwell, The New Yorker, etc.

W.

The next day I sit at Attention under the hypnosis of collating pages when Austra says I have a call: Maxwell.

"Can you come up?" he asks. *They're going to take it*, is my first thought. "We'll look at what I've done to your story and go for lunch. Would sandwiches in Central Park be all right? We'll make it a picnic."

He has gone over the story sentence by sentence, and I'm able to understand what he wants after we go through three or four pages, and he senses that. "Can you work on this in addition to *My Brother's Visit to New York?*"

"Sure, I think."

We sit on a bench in Central Park and he pulls wrapped sandwiches from the paper bag in his lap. I undo mine but can hardly eat. I can't talk; an iron hand lies on my chest and throat. I feel I have to cough but if I cough I'll weep. All he has done presses like a hand of iron and now the time he takes to sit with me, feed me . . . . A pair of swans is circling on the lagoon below as on the cover of an Elizabeth Bowen novel he bought for me to read and I feel choked worse than on the day I tried to ask for a job. The swans in their orbits are my focus and I hear his whispery voice and picture his detailed comments on my pages in his rapid hand and see Bowen's title appear over the swans, *The Death of the Heart.* That is what is happening over this time that feels so endless I'm always able to return to that bench. I turn and his forehead is set with wrinkles of concern, a V dead center, and he pauses, his lips parted, as sometimes happens when he searches for a word, and I can't take in what he's saying, as if pinned to another time.

It is not death but a beginning stirring of life so potent I feel I'll gag on it and then I'm drawn from that by his words falling over me with the force of love. How can I leave? What would I do? Where would I go? We are on a path, then in a cab, and I see how he tips, studying the meter and counting out the exact amount, his concern for the cabby the same as his concern for me; I remember seeing my pages on his table, and then leaving, breath held.

X.

And by that magic transport that can happen in a car, when you're fifty miles farther down the road with not a shred of memory of how you got there, I'm in my room, staring at the pages on my bedside table. Every suggestion of his, every interleaved word in the typed lines shepherds me toward a point I know I have to reach. "Sometimes it feels, I know, like internal bleeding," I hear him say, and look up. It's his voice and I'm not sure if he said it today or another time.

But I hear it now. I follow his trail of pencil marks, feeling chunks of words and paragraphs break loose and fall from the ceiling of my mind, and when I look up, it's dark in the room. My windows multiply me in shiny mirroring plates. I lie down on the bed in all my clothes. *Her.*

y.

I wake with the chilly feeling of a child awakened an hour before sunrise for a fishing trip, when whatever mechanism it is that keeps heat from leaking out of my bones hasn't kicked in yet. I take the closest subway, my usual Lexington line, to Eighty-Sixth and get out in Yorkville, Germantown, Maxwell's neighborhood—he is home for the rest of the week, I know—and as I walk, *O, that towering feeling,* turns in my head, *that o-ver-power-ing feeling! Knowing I'm on the street where you live!*

I walk into Gracie Square, a public park, and notice how the fur on the tail of a squirrel is so fine it appears transparent. I can see through it to the veins of leaves lying in mud, the tail a mirage.

I walk to the river and sit on a green-slatted bench like the one we sat on in the park. The sullen, slow river merges with my senses re-instituting themselves in fall air, as they will every year in commemoration of this day. My life has begun. I will remember every single hour with him. *Mark that down*, I think. *I will do that and I will not relent.* I will return to others, as much as I'm able, a portion of the love he has lavished on me.

Z.

A month later, a story that I draft in one sitting, unrelated to any he has seen, is the first story that the magazine, without a pencil touch from Maxwell, accepts for publication.

ABOUT THE ESSAYS

Part One: *Uses of Words*

"ABCs That Tend to Family Unity" was commissioned in 2008 by CommonBond of
St. Paul, which is, according to its website, "the Upper Midwest's largest non-
profit provider of affordable housing." The piece was intended as preface to
a book of photographs of CommonBond families, but the photographer did
not find it to his liking, although the CommonBond editor did, and promised
to use it elsewhere. It has grown from a one-page preface to a four-page essay.

"Readers' Literary Guide to Litigation" appeared in the form it has here in the
premiere issue of the *Journal of Law and Interdisciplinary Studies*, an Internet
journal launched by the University of North Dakota School of Law (Issue 1,
2011).

"The Worded Flood, Rural to Academy" was commissioned as the introduction to
a poetry anthology edited by James H. Trott, *A Sacrifice of Praise*, published
by Oak and Yew Press, Philadelphia, 1998, and reissued by Cumberland House
Publishing in 1999. I've expanded the original into a minicommentary on college life and poetry.

"Autobiography, Biography, Fiction, and Fact" was presented as a substitute talk
at a Milton Center conference, or as close as memory could cling to its original, "The Uses of Biography, Autobiography, and Fiction as Fact," first given
in 1999 at Union University in Jackson, Tennessee—a substitute because the
talk I intended to give, blossoming in my laptop, was destroyed in a head-on
collision with a pickup that slid into our lane on the way to the Milton Center
conference "Beyond This Weight Is a Boundlessness," at Newman University
in Wichita, Kansas, February, 2000. I've redone the talk for the page and integrated it with a feuilleton titled "The Sides to a Story," included in *F. Scott
Fitzgerald at 100: A Centenary Tribute by American Writers* (privately printed
by Quill & Brush, Rockville, MD, 1996).

"Using Words, a Continual Spiritual Exercise" was first presented at the Colorado
College Symposium on Spirituality & Religion, Colorado Springs, on January,
19, 1994. I've expanded and modified the talk to integrate it with the others.

"Examining the Writer's Image with *IMAGE*" was generated by questions from
the publisher and editor of *Image*, Gregory Wolfe, and the journal's managing
editor, Mary Kenagy Mitchell, and appeared on the *Image* website over the

same season the story, "That Old Dog," was published in *Image: Art, Faith, Mystery* (Fall 2011).

"Pooling Metaphors: On Words Overflowing" was first presented at Wheaton College in 1981 under the title "The Truth of Metaphor"; Beatrice Batson asked to publish it but I couldn't let it go—to be honest, I was hoping to expand it into a book along the lines of Roland Barthes, *really*—and after working on it on-and-off over the years, it appeared in a briefer version than it now has in *Books & Culture* (July-August 1999) under the title "The Word Made Flesh." A condensed version was presented at the Calvin College Festival of Faith and Writing, April 2012.

Part Two: *Users of Words*

"A Fifty-Year Walk with Right Words" was commissioned by Harold Fickett, editor of *Things in Heaven and Earth: Exploring the Supernatural* (Paraclete, 1996), and reappeared, in different form, as "A Fifty-Year Walk" in *Books & Culture* (November-December, 1998); was chosen by Philip Zaleski for inclusion in *The Best Spiritual Writing, 1999* (HarperSanFrancisco); and assumed yet another incarnation as the centerpiece of *What I Think I Did* (Basic, 2000). It has been pruned and smoothed to interlock with the other essays in what I hope is its final form.

"Getting Words Plain Right to Publish" appeared in *Books & Culture* (March-April 1997) under the title "The Maxwell-O'Connor Letters" and I've resisted meddling with it because I heard it gave William Maxwell pleasure near the end of his life.

"Tolstoy's Words March Right to Truth" appeared under the title "How Tolstoy Became Tolstoy," in *Books & Culture* (May-June 1997) and appears with only minor additions and emendations.

"Nabokov's Words Not Fading to Nothing," titled simply "Not Fading to Nothing," also appeared in *Books & Culture* (November-December 1995), over a time when I was doing regular commentary for the publication; I've updated it to include Nabokov titles that have appeared since, under the editorship of Nabokov's son, Dmitri.

"Exchanging Words: Aural Northern Lights" was written as a chapter for the novel *Born Brothers*, but had to go as the novel grew, besides being too explicit for fiction, as I judged, and appeared under the title "Dispositions," in *Northern Lights: Studies in Creativity*, published by the University of Maine at Presque Isle, 1983. I've pared down the dialogue and added contemporary allusions.

"With *Inside*'s Words inside SUNY Academy" is an interview that took place in my office at SUNY-Binghamton where I was serving on the creative-writing faculty and staring at a recorder placed between me and the interviewer, Hal Smith, 1984. I gave up my tenured position to return to North Dakota.

"Words at the Last from a Martyr Who Lives" was commissioned by Susan Bergman for *Martyrs: Contemporary Writers on Modern Lives of Faith* (HarperSan-Francisco, 1996) and appeared in that collection under the title, "A Martyr Who Lives;" under the same title in *Books & Culture* (March-April, 1996); and in a condensed version in *New Horizons* (February 1998), the official publication of the Orthodox Presbyterian Church.

Part Three: *Realms of Users*

"A State Laureate's Graduation Address" adheres partly to an address—whenever Brodsky is mentioned—given at Geneva College (Beaver, Pennsylvania) for its 1997 graduation ceremony; the earlier history of the office of poet laureate I've added, as I wanted to that evening, because I'm often asked, "What is a poet laureate?" and Brodsky the Russian served as America's national laureate.

"A Concern for the State of Indian Affairs" was prepared for a cultural tour under the auspices of the US State Department at a time when Canada was consider-ing the disposition of its First Nations and the establishment of Nunavit, the year my novel *Indian Affairs* (Atheneum, 1992) appeared; I delivered versions of "The State of Indian Affairs," at the universities of Ottawa, Toronto, Alberta, Manitoba, McGill, the National Library, and spoke on CBC, Chez Radio, and other venues over October and November, 1992; I've since pared down portions of the talk, expanded others, and updated several references, including a letter of 2005 addressed to an English Department in the United States.

"A View of the Ethics Related to Writing" was the keynote address at the World Journalism Institute's June term closing banquet (New York City, June 27, 2003). The Institute offers courses and internships in New York for college-age Christian writers, and their banquet was held at the Algonquin Hotel on the above date; the Institute later published the talk as a chapbook, http://www.worldji.com/resources/view/40, and the interspersed headings and footnotes in the online version are theirs.

"A Turn in Aesthetics as a Century Turns" was presented at the September 2000 *Veritas* conference, sponsored by the Center for Christian Study at the Univer-sity of Virginia, Charlotte, under the title, "Openings to Aesthetics."

"A Final Meeting at the Algonquin Hotel" was composed in a seizure of hilarity generated by two months of freedom to work as I wished (when I also drafted a novel, I should note) at Marfa, Texas, in a house of my own, on a generous Lannan Foundation Residency Fellowship. It was 2003, before iPads and the like existed, and two publications that showed interest in the piece said it was too long, so I pared it down (I've pared it further and added updated references), and by then my agent seemed nervous about sending it around, so it appears here for the first time.

"A View on Writing from Another Country" was called into being by questions faxed to me in London by the duo mentioned in a note, who were then co-editors of *Image*, although the interview was for *The World & I* magazine (Vol. 3. No. 9, September, 1988) and appeared with a generous excerpt from the novel, *Born Brothers,* along with accompanying essays that are without exception the most discerning examinations of my work in general, by Gregory Wolfe, and in particular, by Harold Fickett, who discloses the novel's structure and intent with the ease of genius. I've let the interview stand as it appeared, smoothing only time-bound distractions, and was surprised to find that in 1988 I made statements such as "the most violent and radical practitioners of Islam are lumped, along with any American who reads the Bible, as 'fundamentalists,'" etc.

"A Writer's Feel of Internal Bleeding, A to Z" was excerpted from a 1999 manuscript of *What I Think I Did* and included by the editor John Wilson in *The Best Christian Writing, 2000* (New York: HarperSanFrancisco). It appears here with alphabetic steps but otherwise as it did in that anthology in order to sign off these words on a note of faith and hope about a man of charity.

NOTES

CHAPTER 1: ABCs THAT TEND TO FAMILY UNITY

1. Gerald Locklin, "Un Bel Di," in Garrison Keillor, *Good Poems, American Places* (New York: Viking, 2011), 238–39.

CHAPTER 2: READERS' LITERARY GUIDE TO LITIGATION

1. Graham Greene, "Two Friends," in *Collected Essays* (New York: Penguin, 1970), 60–62; unless otherwise indicated, all following quotations are from this essay.

2. My emphasis.

3. Henry James, *The Art of the Novel: Critical Prefaces* (New York: Charles Scribner's and Sons, 1934).

CHAPTER 3: THE WORDED FLOOD, RURAL TO ACADEMY

1. James H. Trott, ed., *A Sacrifice of Praise: An Anthology of Christian Poetry in English from Caedmon to the Mid-Twentieth Century*, 2nd ed. (Nashville: Cumberland, 2006).

CHAPTER 4: AUTOBIOGRAPHY, BIOGRAPHY, FICTION, AND FACT

1. Charles Johnson, "Fiction and the Liberation of Perception" on E-Channel: "The Words and Wisdom of Charles Johnson," a website creation of E. Ethelbert Miller, June 1, 2011, http://www.ethelbert-miller.blogspot.com/. Accessed November 23, 2012. This project, which will appear in eBook format by Dzanc and covers an entire calendar year, prints out to 512 pages (project information provided in an e-mail from Charles Johnson, November 22, 2012).

2. John Gardner, *On Moral Fiction* (New York: Basic, 1977), 100.

3. William Maxwell, "The Autobiographical Novelist," (lecture, Arts Festival, University of Illinois, Urbana, 1963). No typescript or copy of this talk, as far as is known at the present, exists.

4. Johnson, "Fiction and the Liberation of Perception," http://www.ethelbert-miller.blogspot.com/.

5. This and other companionable addresses are scattered through Ivan Turgenev's *Sportsman's Sketches*, also titled *A Sportsman's Notebook*, trans. Charles and Natasha Hepburn, Compass Books ed. (New York: Viking, 1957), as in "Tatyana Borisovna and Her Nephew," and Turgenev's companionable tone may have been meant to ingratiate or disarm the general reader, because Turgenev was the first Russian fiction writer to include serfs as human beings in his writing.

6. Ernest Hemingway, "Hawks Do Not Share," in *A Moveable Feast* (New York: Charles Scribner's Sons, 1964), 186.

7. Ernest Hemingway, "The Snows of Kilimanjaro," 1930.

8. Fitzgerald to Hemingway, Asheville, 16 July 1936, in Matthew J. Bruccoli,

Scott and Ernest: The Authority of Failure and the Authority of Success (New York: Random, 1978), 131.

9. William Shakespeare, *Hamlet*, ed. David Bevington (New York: Pearson Longman, 2004), 2.2.192. References are to act, scene, and line.

CHAPTER 5: USING WORDS, A CONTINUAL SPIRITUAL EXERCISE

1. William James, *The Varieties of Religious Experience*, First Library of America Paperback Classics ed. (New York: Literary Classics of the United States, 2010), 438.

2. W. B. Yeats, "The Second Coming," line 3.

3. Unsigned review, "The Canker in the Rose," of *What I'm Going to Do, I Think*, by L. Woiwode, *Time* (June 20, 1969): 89–90.

4. William Blake, "To God," in *The Complete Writings of William Blake*, ed. Geoffrey Keynes (London: Oxford University Press, 1966), 557.

5. *Born Brothers* (New York: Farrar, Straus & Giroux, 1988), 32.

6. *Acts: A Writer's Reflection on the Church, Writing, and His Own Life* (New York: HarperSanFrancisco, 1993), 5.

7. *Beyond the Bedroom Wall* (New York: Farrar, Straus & Giroux, 1975), 256.

8. Ibid., 97.

9. *Acts*, 82.

10. *Born Brothers*, 219.

CHAPTER 6: EXAMINING THE WRITER'S IMAGE WITH *IMAGE*

1. Larry Woiwode, "That Old Dog," *Image* 71 (Fall 2011): 7–16.

CHAPTER 7: POOLING METAPHORS: ON WORDS OVERFLOWING

1. John 14:6 and John 17:17.

2. Samuel Taylor Coleridge, "Kubla Khan," *The Oxford Book of English Verse*, ed. Sir Arthur Quiller-Couch (New York-Toronto: Oxford University Press, 1939), 668.

3. William Shakespeare, *As You Like It*, ed. David Bevington (New York: Pearson Longman, 2004), 2.7.138. References are to act, scene, and line.

4. William Shakespeare, *Macbeth*, ed. David Bevington (New York: Pearson Longman, 2004), 5.5.24–26.

5. Vladimir Nabokov, *Ada* (New York: McGraw-Hill, 1969), 571.

6. The lines I refer to appeared in stanzas two through four in part III of "In Memory of W. B. Yeats" and were later excised by Auden. Auden's literary executor, Edward Mendelson, speculates that the excisions Auden performed on several poems later in life were due to his growing sensitivity to aesthetics and ethics, although in "historical" interest Mendelson preserves the lines in *Selected Poems*. The stanzas as they originally appeared, including stanza one of part III, run this way:

III
Earth receive an honored guest
William Yeats is laid to rest;
Let the Irish vessel lie
Emptied of its poetry.

[Time that is intolerant
Of the brave and innocent
And indifferent in a week
To a beautiful physique,

Worships language and forgives
Everyone by whom it lives;
Pardons cowardice, conceit,
Lays its honors at their feet.

Time that with this strange excuse
Pardoned Kipling and his views,
And will pardon Paul Claudel,
Pardons him for writing well.]

The first of the excised stanzas may have been dropped for aesthetic reasons. Joseph Brodsky, in his commentary on the poem in "To Please a Shadow" (*Less Than One* [NY: Farrar, Straus & Giroux, 1986], 362) said that the tetrameter lines "sound like a cross between a Salvation Army hymn, a funeral dirge, and a nursery rhyme"—while I hear the smacking action of a spade busy at January soil to open a grave; no backhoes in Ireland in 1939. The third stanza may have bothered ethical Auden in its slights of two poets; even if the reader nods and agrees with a smile, the slights can't be seen as charitable. Then what could Auden do with the remaining lines of the stanzas except drop them? If we begin with the word "Time" and leave off the defining examples to arrive at the central verb, time "worships language and forgives / Everyone by whom it lives," we have a statement the Nobel Laureate Brodsky found remarkable, as I do, and it's regrettable Auden couldn't somehow preserve it.

(Stanza one of part III quoted from Richard Aldington, ed., *The Viking Book of Poetry of the English-Speaking World*, rev. ed. [New York: Viking, 1958], 2:1230.)

7. Bob Dylan, "Time Passes Slowly," *Lyrics, 1962–2001* (New York: Simon & Schuster, 2004), 259.

8. John Gardner, *The Art of Fiction: Notes on Craft for Young Writers* (New York: Alfred A. Knopf, 1984), 31ff.

9. Bob Dylan, "The Times They Are A-Changin'," *Lyrics, 1962–2001*, 81.

10. Randall Jarrell, "An Unread Book," *The Third Book of Criticism* (New York: Farrar, Straus & Giroux, 1965), 50.

11. John Updike, *Bech: A Book* (New York: Alfred A. Knopf, 1970), 141.

12. Erik H. Erikson, *Gandhi's Truth* (New York: W. W. Norton, 1969), 180.

13. Christopher Marlowe, *Doctor Faustus*, in *The Norton Anthology of English Literature,* ed. Stephen Greenblatt et al, 8th ed. (New York: W. W. Norton, 2006), 1:1054, scene 13, lines 70–71.

14. H. R. Rookmaaker, *Modern Art and the Death of a Culture* (London: Inter-Varsity, 1970), 30–31.

15. Ibid., 32.

Notes

CHAPTER 8: A FIFTY-YEAR WALK WITH RIGHT WORDS

1. Psalm 19:1–3; Romans 1:20; Colossians 1:16–17 (NKJV).
2. Joseph Brodsky, "To Please a Shadow," *Less Than One: Selected Essays* (New York: Farrar, Straus & Giroux, 1986), 363.
3. Ibid.
4. *Beyond the Bedroom Wall* (New York: Farrar, Straus & Giroux, 1975), 8.

CHAPTER 9: GETTING WORDS PLAIN RIGHT TO PUBLISH

1. Michael Steinman, ed., *The Happiness of Getting It Down Right: Letters of Frank O'Connor and William Maxwell* (New York: Alfred A. Knopf, 1996).
2. Ibid., 14–15.
3. V. S. Pritchett, review of *My Father's Son* by Frank O'Connor, *New York Times Book Review* 74 (November 16, 1969), 3.
4. William Maxwell, *So Long, See You Tomorrow* (New York: Alfred A. Knopf, 1980), dust jacket, hardback 1st edition.
5. William Maxwell, "Frank O'Connor and *The New Yorker*," in Steinman, *Happiness*, 263–70; quote, 265.
6. Letter from Frank O'Connor to William Maxwell, Bucks, England, 5 March 1954, 25–26.
7. Letter from William Maxwell to Frank O'Connor, New York, 10 March 1954, 27.
8. William Maxwell, ed., *Letters: Sylvia Townsend Warner* (London: Chatto & Windus, 1982), *viii*.
9. Letter from Willaim Maxwell to Frank O'Connor, New York, 10 March 1954, 27.
10. Letter from Frank O'Connor to William Maxwell, Annapolis, late April 1956, 52.
11. Letter from William Maxwell to Harriet O'Connor, New York, 12 June 1958, 82.
12. Letter from William Maxwell to Frank O'Connor, New York, 6 January 1965, 230.
13. Letter from William Maxwell to Frank O'Connor, New York, 6 July 1956, 57–58.
14. Letter from Frank O'Connor to William Maxwell, Annapolis, 7 July 1986, 58.
15. Telegram from William Maxwell to Frank O'Connor, New York, 29 May 1956, 54.
16. Letter from William Maxwell to Frank O'Connor, New York, early June 1956, 54–55.
17. Letter from William Maxwell to Frank O'Connor, New York, before 19 May 1955, 38.

CHAPTER 10: TOLSTOY'S WORDS MARCH RIGHT TO TRUTH

1. Kathryn B. Feuer, *Tolstoy and the Genesis of "War and Peace"*, ed. Robin Feuer Miller and Donna Tussing Orwin (Ithaca, NY: Cornell University Press, 1966).
2. Nicholas V. Riasanovsky, *A History of Russia*, 4th ed. (New York–Oxford: Oxford University Press, 1984), 373–74. See also Feuer, *Tolstoy and the Genesis*, 26n2.

3. Luke 9:23 and Philippians 1:29.

4. C. S. Lewis, *The Weight of Glory and Other Addresses* (Grand Rapids, MI: Eerdmans, 1975), 14–15.

CHAPTER 18: A TURN IN AESTHETICS AS A CENTURY TURNS

1. Andrew Sullivan, "Enemies, A Love Story" *New York Times* (April 16, 2000): 28.

2. Ibid.

3. Ibid.

4. Ibid.

5. Ibid.

6. Ibid., 30.

7. Marilynne Robinson, "Darwinism," *The Death of Adam: Essays on Modern Thought* (Boston: Houghton Mifflin, 1998), 27.

8. Calvin Seerveld, *Rainbows for a Fallen World* (Downsview, Ontario: Toronto Tuppence, 1980).

9. Anthony Burgess, *English Literature: A Survey for Students* (London: Longman, 1979), 2–3.

10. Katherine Anne Porter, afterword to Willa Cather, *The Troll Garden* (New York: New American Library, 1961), 148.

11. Ibid., 149–50.

12. Robert Pirsig, *LILA: An Inquiry into Morals* (New York: Bantam, 1991), 323.

13. W. H. Auden, "In Memory of W. B. Yeats," in *Collected Poems*, ed. Edward Mendelson (New York: Modern Library, 2007), 245, line 27.

14. Robinson, "Darwinism," 42.

15. Ibid., 43.

16. Ibid.

17. Ibid., 58–59.

18. Lawrence Weschler, "The Looking Glass," *New Yorker* (January 31, 2000): 64.

19. Robinson, "Darwinism," 70–71.

20. Daphne Merkin, "Trouble in the Tribe," *New Yorker* (September 11, 2000): 52.

21. John Donne, "Holy Sonnet XV," in *The Poems of John Donne*, ed. Sir Herbert Grierson (London-New York: Oxford University Press, 1964), 300.

CHAPTER 19: A FINAL MEETING AT THE ALGONQUIN HOTEL

1. "Writer Roth Honored in His Hometown," *Bismarck Tribune* (Bismark, ND), October 25, 2005.

CHAPTER 20: A VIEW ON WRITING FROM ANOTHER COUNTRY

1. The inquisitors for *The World & I* are Harold Fickett and Gregory Wolfe, then coeditors of *Image*. The interview appeared in September 1988.

2. Galatians 5:11.

3. Proverbs 29:18 KJV.

4. Psalm 100:1.

It's up to writers, as it's been for centuries,
to help us find our way around this home on earth,
whatever our place on it.

—*Larry Woiwode*

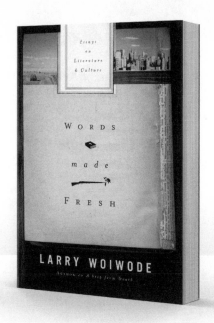

Each of Woiwode's 10 essays in *Words Made Fresh* seems a kind
of heirloom, important and timeless, a real window into the soul of
American culture and its literary figures.

"This stunning collection of thought and prose has made me think
and dream as I haven't in years."

G. W. HAWKES, *Professor of English, Lycoming College*

"Larry Woiwode's prose is so piercing and precise, so concrete and
muscular, that I would read his reflections on the price of potatoes."

GREGORY WOLFE, *writer in residence, Seattle Pacific University*

Notes

3. Feuer, *Tolstoy and the Genesis*, 86n3.
4. Ibid., 48.
5. Ibid., 193.
6. From Ibid., 130n252, quoting *Polnoe sobranie sochinenii;* Complete Collected Works, XIII, 245.
7. From Ibid., 131n252, quoting *Voina I mir*, the published *War and Peace*.

CHAPTER 11: NABOKOV'S WORDS NOT FADING TO NOTHING

1. Letter from Vladmir Nabokov to his mother, Berlin, 1925 in Brian Boyd, *The Russian Years* (Princeton, NJ: Princeton University Press, 1990), 1:239.
2. Vladimir Nabokov, "Beneficence," *The Stories of Vladimir Nabokov*, ed. Dimtri Nabokov (New York: Alfred A. Knopf, 1995), 77.
3. Theodore Roethke, "I Knew a Woman," in *The Collected Verse of Theodore Roethke* (Bloomington, IN: Indiana University Press, 1963), 151 line 4.
4. Nabokov, "La Veneziana," *Stories*, 105.
5. Nabokov, "A Letter That Never Reached Russia," *Stories*, 138.
6. Ibid., 140.
7. Nabokov, "A Guide to Berlin," *Stories*, 157.
8. Nabokov, "Notes," *Stories*, 639–51.
9. Nabokov, "Lance," *Stories*, 635.
10. Ibid.
11. Vladimir Nabokov, *Pale Fire* (New York: Putnam, 1962), 227.

CHAPTER 12: EXCHANGING WORDS: AURAL NORTHERN LIGHTS

1. Psalm 139:15–16.
2. William Wordsworth, "The Rainbow," *The Oxford Book of English Verse*, ed. Sir Arthur Quiller-Couch (New York-Toronto: Oxford University Press, 1939), 624.

CHAPTER 13: WITH *INSIDE*'S WORDS INSIDE SUNY ACADEMY

1. The interviewer is Hal Smith, editor of *Inside*, a publication of the State University of New York, Binghamton.

CHAPTER 14: WORDS AT THE LAST FROM A MARTYR WHO LIVES

1. Transcriptions of Men's radio broadcasts were supplied to me, in translation, by Susan Bergman the editor who commissioned this piece for *Martyrs: Contemporary Writers on Modern Faith* (San Francisco: HarperSanFrancisco, 1996).
2. Many videos and memorials on Aleksandr Men are available now on the Internet, as they were not a decade ago. Observers of the websites will note that in recent years a movement has been growing in the Orthodox Church to officially designate Men an ordained saint.
3. Renamed for a revolutionary, the city has now returned to its former name: Serfeev Posad. Yves Hamant, *Alexander Men: A Witness for Contemporary Russia (A Man for Our Times)*, trans. Steven Bigham, (Torrance, CA: Oakwood, 1995), 37.
4. Michael Meerson, "The Life and Work of Father Aleksandr Men'," in *Seeking God: The Recovery of Religious Identity in Orthodox Russia, and Georgia*, ed. Stephen Batalden (DeKalb, IL: Northern Illinois University Press, 1993), 13–17, 20. I have also drawn heavily on Meerson's chapter for the facts of Men's

life. From all I've sorted through, Meerson seems (given my admittedly imperfect perspective) to be the most consistently accurate. Other aids have been the article from *Frontier* quoted; Mark Elliot's reports from the Institute for the Study of Christianity and Marxism; News Network International reports; and the Keston News Service of Keston College in Kent, England.

5. Ibid., 19.

6. See http://www.roca.org/OA/103/103e.htm for a similar quote. All of these arrive in translation.

7. Meerson, "The Life and Work,"14.

8. Ibid., 11. The issue of *Frontier* magazine for January–March, 1993, contains a similar reconstruction, with varying details, of Men's slaying.

9. Francis X. Clines, "Slain Soviet Priest: Victim of Martyr?" *New York Times*, September 15, 1992, http://www.nytimes.com/1990/09/15/world/slain-soviet-priest-victim-of-martyr.html.

10. Revelation 1:18 NKJV.

CHAPTER 15: A STATE LAUREATE'S GRADUATION ADDRESS

1. Joseph Brodsky, "A Commencement Address," in *Less Than One: Selected Essays* (New York: Farrar, Straus & Giroux, 1986), 385.

2. I am thinking, first, of Shakespeare, who set the drama of the Christian life incarnate onstage, of Donne, the military man turned Reformed poetic Christian preacher; and the growing force of the Reformation itself: Luther versus Erasmus.

3. Brodsky, "A Commencement Address," 385.

4. Ibid., 387–89.

CHAPTER 16: A CONCERN FOR THE STATE OF INDIAN AFFAIRS

1. Rudy Wiebe, *The Temptations of Big Bear* (Toronto: McClelland & Stewart, 1973; New Canadian Library, 1976), 44–45.

2. James Welch, *Fools Crow* (New York: Penguin, 1987), 279. The new edition (2011) has an introduction by Thomas McGuane.

3. Stephen Crane, "The Open Boat," *The Heath Anthology of American Literature: Concise Edition*, eds. Paul Lauter, et al. (Boston-New York: Houghton Mifflin, 2004), 1557.

4. Wiebe, *The Temptations of Big Bear*, 36–37.

5. Welch, *Fools Crow*, 199.

6. Ibid., 323.

7. Ibid.

8. John Wain, *Samuel Johnson* (New York: Viking, 1975), 46.

9. Michael Dorris and Louise Erdrich, *The Crown of Columbus* (New York: HarperCollins, 1991), 374.

10. Wain, *Samuel Johnson*, 46.

CHAPTER 17: A VIEW OF THE ETHICS RELATED TO WRITING

1. James R. Edwards, "Glorifying God in All Things," *The Edwards Epistle* 12, no.1 (Spring 2003).

2. Alan Bloom, *The Closing of the American Mind* (New York: Simon & Schuster, 1987), 25.